"IT CAN BE DONE"

The Hundred Year History
of the
1st Norwich Sea Scout Group

Researched and written by Jane Stafford and Rhonda Pike

About the Authors

Jane Stafford

Jane has spent the last four years, researching the history of the Group and gathering material for the book. She researched the extensive archive, collected stories from many past and present Scouts and their families, and scanned and sorted through the thousands of photographs that document the life of the Group over the past hundred years.

Jane has made many friends through Scouting. She became involved when her eldest son, Chris became a Cub. She is married to Reg, has two married sons, two step children and four grandchildren. One of her greatest Scouting moments was investing her granddaughter Megan into the Group as a Beaver Scout. Other highlights include the trip to Poland with the Scouts in 1994 and attending the 21st World Scout Jamboree.

Rhonda Pike

Rhonda's family has been involved in Scouting since her daughter (later a Queen's Guide) joined the Brownies in 1976. Her two sons were 1st Norwich Sea Scouts in the 1980s and one of them, Julien, subsequently became Scout Leader from 1991 to 1995. Her husband, Graham, was Chairman of the Parents Committee for a time.

Having volunteered to help Jane with this project by attempting to bring order to what initially appeared to be an unmanageable mountain of information she carried out further research on the archive and wrote much of the text.

Acknowledgements

Our thanks must go to the many people who helped in the writing of this book including all the past and present 1st Norwich Group Members and others who contributed memories, recollections and photographs.

In particular, we thank Terry Marshall for doing the layout, Andrew Hawker for proof reading and advice, and finally our families, especially Reg and Graham, for their continued help and support.

Forward

I was delighted to read the long and interesting history of the 1st Norwich Scout Group. I wonder if our Founder Robert Baden-Powell had any idea what he would start when he agreed to write 'Scouting for Boys'. Sitting in his study in 1907 he wrote a number of ideas and then developed them into a fortnightly series of small leaflets for boys to read and 'have a go at'.

Now 100 years later the 1st Norwich Scout Group are celebrating their centenary and it is humbling to think back on the countless thousands of young people who have been part of the Group over these last 100 years. These young people have been supported by many adults who from the early support of Mr and Mrs Glover to today's leadership team have given their services free of charge and for many have given their annual holidays to ensure that the Scouts had a camping experience.

The pages tell of the growth and development of the Group and the main players along the way. The many adventures they have undertaken and the part they have played in the lives of the young people and their leaders.

I congratulate all involved in this great achievement and wish you all well as you move into the second century of serving the young people of Norwich. Cardinal Newman that great Victorian said *'Growth is the only evidence of life'* and the 1st have grown into a modern Scout Group serving local children. They have kept up with the changes to the movement and they ensure that Scouting is as relevant today as it was on the 15th January 1908 when those two school boys met and without knowing it started a long story and one that is still being told today.

Gods speed to you all on the continued journey.

Richard M Butler DL
County Commissioner

ISBN 978-0-9561286-0-7

Published by
1st Norwich Sea Scout Group
13 Old Lakenham Hall Drive,
Old Lakenham, Norwich, Norfolk, NR1 2NW

www.firstnorwichseascouts.co.uk

Registered Charity Number: 1034608

Printed in England by Barnwell Print Ltd,
Dunkirk, Aylsham, Norfolk NR11 6SU. T: 01263 732767

Care has been taken to ensure the accuracy of information contained in this book. If names, dates or
places are incorrect, please contact the 1st Norwich Scout Group so the record can be amended.

All profits from the sale of 'It Can Be Done' will go to the 1st Norwich Sea Scout Group.

Front cover photograph: *Top, Chief Scout, Sir Robert Baden-Powell, travels in the War Canoe from
Thorpe Station to Pulls Ferry, 1926.*
Bottom, Beavers, Cubs, Scouts and Explorers form a 'Human 100' on City Hall steps, January 2008.
Back cover photograph: *The Group on City Hall steps, St George's Day. April 2007.*

Contents

Early Days 1908-14.

Lion Patrol

One wintry morning on the 15th of January, 1908, two schoolboys of Norwich School met in the quadrangle … They each noticed that the other was looking at a …pamphlet by Lt. Gen. Robert Baden-Powell … It was the first fortnightly part of Scouting for Boys … We were both late for morning prayers, but that meeting and discussion were to have far-reaching results. We agreed to form a Boy Scout Patrol with Lawrence Glover as Patrol Leader and myself as 'Corporal' and we decided to call it the Lion Patrol. This was the foundation stone of the 1st Norwich Troop. (Extract from Edward (Skipper) Coe's Memoirs)

Four other boys joined the patrol and they met weekly at Cliff House, the home of Lawrence Glover, whose father was manager of the Gas Works. The Scouts pooled two thirds of their pocket money to buy patrol equipment, and in their enthusiasm for Scouting soon increased their meetings to three times a week.

They received support and encouragement from Mr and Mrs Glover, who gave them full use of the small copse in the grounds of Cliff House. Skipper Coe described the copse as a Scout's paradise with

…all kinds of trees, plenty of undergrowth, blackberry bushes and on its outskirts masses of bracken.

Clumps of nettles were a little unkind to the exposed portions of our legs, but when they died gave us tinder for our fires. That phrase in Scouting for Boys, 'lay and light a fire using no more than two matches', soon taught us that even with dead nettle stems, green wood will not burn. Eventually, we mastered the technique and even got to the stage when we scorned the use of two matches and lit our fire with one match, halved.

Early Activities of Lion Patrol

Following instructions given by Baden-Powell in Scouting for Boys, the Scouts quickly mastered new activities and passed the tests required to gain their Second Class Badges. Some of these activities were:

First Aid

Mrs Glover instructed the Scouts in elementary First Aid. They learnt how to bandage, dress minor wounds and treat small ailments, and they were rewarded for their efforts with … *cakes, buns, pastries and lemonade.*

Pioneering

First efforts saw the patrol building a hut by cutting a single pole, leaning it against a tree and thatching it with branches and brushwood. The result was a reasonably waterproof shelter that stood for nearly six months but was eventually used for firewood.

They tested the shelter using a hose and drew lots to decide who would be inside when the hose was turned on. Edward Coe lost

… and forthwith was compelled to enter the hut while the rest enjoyed the fun. Being disappointed that I emerged comparatively dry they greeted me with a shower bath which soaked me to the skin.

Edward Coe as a young Scout.

Knotting

The Scouts found a naval Petty Officer to teach them knotting and splicing. Starting with the reef knot they progressed on to other tenderfoot knots such as the sheet bend, clove hitch, bowline, round turn and two half hitches and the sheepshank. They practised tying knots behind their backs as well as in the dark and

… to improve our speed each Scout was given two nine foot lashings, which he used to tie all the tenderfoot knots round and about his body …The record was …forty-five seconds.

Semaphore and Boxing the Compass

Under the instruction of the same naval officer the group were able to send and receive messages by semaphore after only a few weeks of practice. They also learnt to set a map and find north using the position of the sun and a watch.

First Camp

In the hope of being allowed to go on a weekend camp without adult supervision, the boys invited their parents to a Patrol meeting where they … *pitched a tent and then cooked a meal of sausages and mashed potatoes followed by a pot of tea.* The parents judged the meal as … *good though a trifle smoked* and reluctantly gave their consent to a weekend camp which took place in the late summer of 1908. Skipper Coe describes this as their first great adventure:

Equipped with dixies, raw meat, potatoes, salt, and hopeful anticipation, we went to Stoke Holy Cross, collected firewood, and made our first attempt at cooking in the open. The result was hardly an unqualified success, the meat was tough and our experiment was rudely interrupted by the Bussey brothers, whose father had allowed us the use of the site.

Our first indication of their presence was a large lump of hard clay which demolished our fire and upset the dixies. We staged a counter attack and finally captured their ammunition dump, a small clay pit. Armed with hastily fashioned balls of clay we routed the enemy who retired to the safety of their base.

We rescued what was left of our stew, and sat down to consume it, only to be attacked again, this time with a bombardment of walnuts. We rather enjoyed this because the walnuts were edible and made a tasty dessert. Hostilities ceased and in the afternoon we fraternised with our erstwhile enemies.

One of the brothers, Alec Bussey subsequently joined the Scout Movement and went on to found the 2nd Norwich Troop, of which he was Scout Master until his death in 1953.

Kangaroo Patrol

When the Coe family moved to Unthank Road in late 1908 Edward Coe started the Kangaroos, a new patrol. With himself as Leader, his brother Geoffrey as Corporal and five other boys, they met in a shed at the bottom of the Coes' garden and soon all gained their Second Class Badges.

A patrol diary, written by Edward Coe in late 1909, illustrates the activities of the patrol and tells of contact with General Baden-Powell on his visit to Norwich.

*A camp in 1909. Left to right, standing: Burrell, Dye, ?.
Seated: Thorn, C F Bower, E Coe.*

Baden-Powell Boy Scouts 1st Norwich Troop

At some time in 1909 the two patrols became attached to the CEYMS Troop. They were now officially known as the Baden-Powell Boy Scouts 1st Norwich Troop, with Mr Claude Stratford as Scout Master and Mr Charles Bower as Assistant Scout Master.

First Class Badge

In August, Edward Coe attended the camp organised by Baden-Powell at Buckler's Hard in Hampshire. One hundred places had been awarded as prizes in a competition published in The Scout Magazine. Boys had the opportunity to spend a week on the training ship Mercury and a week camping on land. While at the camp Edward Coe had the distinction of being presented with his First Class badge by Baden-Powell.

CEYMS Troop, to whom the 1st Norwich were attached in 1909.

Inspection by the King

Ten members of 1st Norwich were invited to form part of the guard of honour when King Edward VII visited Norwich on October 25th 1909. They paraded on St Andrew's Plain, formed up at the entrance to St Andrew's Hall, and were among 120 Scouts inspected by the King.

Later in the day, they formed up alongside Norfolk veterans on the parade ground at the Military Barracks at Mousehold while the King presented Colours to units of the Norfolk Territorials.

In preparation for the event the Scouts had attended early morning drilling practices at the Barracks. As a result, their proficiency and general behaviour earned them compliments from the military officers. Skipper Coe, however, remembered that after lunch and a lot of waiting around, discipline was somewhat weakened.

When the time came for the boys to be on parade again they

... formed up in a rather ragged square and stood at ease. Suddenly a terrified rabbit came out of its burrow, gave one startled look at all those bare knees and scuttled across the square. Discipline went to the wind ...and practically every Scout gave chase. The rabbit escaped, but they were very chastened Scouts who returned in time to receive a very justified reprimand and to re-form their ranks.

Drill at the Artillery Barracks, 1910.

On the march back home the Scouts were unfortunately subjected to derogatory remarks from bystanders because of their uniform of shorts, stockings, hats and staves.

Early Opposition

The Scout Movement was not universally accepted when it first started. Some people believed it to be a military movement and the uniform appeared strange to the general public.

The boys of Lion patrol had met with opposition locally in the form of ridicule and even physical violence. Skipper Coe says they had many fights to retain their badges. He remembered

... one particular nuisance who, with his pals, made our lives a misery by constant bullying, until one day we challenged them and a really rough free-for-all ensued. We were a bit smaller than they and although we gave a good account of ourselves we got somewhat knocked about. When all had had enough, I suggested that we shake hands and this they grudgingly did. No more trouble occurred and we continued our existence on terms of peaceful neutrality.

Support developed over time but Scouts continued to meet with opposition, sometimes from their teachers and fellow pupils at school. In February 1910 when the Norwich School Debating Society considered the motion that 'This house approves of the Boy Scout Movement,' the motion was lost by twelve votes.

First Norfolk King's Scout

Edward Coe was awarded his King's Scout badge in May 1910, the first in Norfolk.

On October 26th. We went to Mr Hotchins, Stacy and Andrews being present. First there was a despatch run from the end of the lane to the camp. Coe 2 was despatch runner, he was caught by Coe 1, about 5 yards from the camp. We then collected wood and kindled a fire and had our tea. We then cleared up and marched to our bicycles.

On October 30th. There was an inspection at the Drill Hall. The Chief Scout came to inspect us and the whole of the Patrol was present. First the Chief Scout inspected us, then there was a short service, after which Baden-Powell addressed the Scouts. He said he was very pleased with the Scouts, that he was coming again soon and hoped to see more badges. He was also very pleased with our Ambulance Patrol, who, he said, were covered with badges. We then marched to the CEYMS Rooms and dismissed.

On November 14th. The Patrol was invited to Mr Stratford to tea. We were all present except Boston 1 and 2. We got there at six and had tea at 5 minutes past, we had a good feed, which Mr Stratford had prepared for us. Then we had games of Halma and Draughts. Mr Stratford offered 6d to the Scout who did a certain puzzle in 10 minutes, but none of us succeeded. Then at about a quarter to eight we all went home.

Extract from the diary of Kangaroo Patrol, 1909.

Outside St Thomas Church Hall, Earlham Rd., 1913.
Left to right. Back row: Cushion, Middleton, Cox.
2nd row: A Towers, ?, Baker, Bishop, Spalding.
Leaders: Hayden, Bower. Sitting front: C Markham, Campling,
Haggar, F Markham.

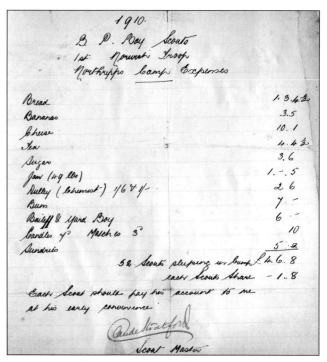

Camp expenses at Northrepps, 1910.

St Thomas' (1st Norwich) Troop

In 1912, the 1st Norwich Troop became St Thomas' (1st Norwich) Troop with Charles Bower as Scout Master. They met in St Thomas' church hall on Earlham Road.

Charles Bower had become a warranted Scout Master in October 1911. Records show that for a time, he was Scoutmaster of the Norwich Grammar School Troop but do not indicate how it was related to the 1st Norwich Troop. The School Troop met in the early mornings and at lunchtimes and also attended weekly sessions at the 'Club-house' in the grounds of Edward Coe's family home, 'Homestead' in Unthank Road.

Camping under supervision

From the time of their attachment to the CEYMS Troop the boys of Lion and Kangaroo patrols had adult supervision when they went camping. A summer camp was held in August 1909 for eight Scouts. A list of orders was drawn up and two orderlies appointed each day. They had the task of fetching water from the well and checking that the camp-site and tents had been tidied up. All Scouts were required to be on the look-out for Good Turns to perform and to help one another.

Northrepps

In April 1910 fifty-two Scouts under Claude Stratford, Scout Master of the CEYMS Troop, camped at Northrepps in a barn lent by Mr Quintin Gurney. The cost for each Scout was one shilling and eight pence. The journey to Cromer was made either by train or bicycle, six pence being the return train fare. Scouts were given a list of the kit they should take and parents were assured that ... *every care would be taken against Scouts getting wet.*

1st Norwich Troop at the Chief Scout's Rally,
Crown Point. June 1914.

Group photo, May 1914.
Left to right, standing: H Cooper, D Robinson, W Shorten, S Spalding, W H Middleton,
T Towers, A Towers, J Osbourne.
Middle row: J E G Mosby, E H Coe, C J Bower, W Cox, F Bennett.
Front: L Anderson, S Potter, R Nudd, R Spall, W Savage, R Springett, W Sadd.

A year later, in August 1912, when they went back to Sea Palling the boys were asked not to bring sardines to camp. This camp was memorable because of the great floods of that year. The camp was flooded out with tents marooned in a foot of water.

Benacre 1913
In 1913 Scouts camped with a patrol from the 2nd Norwich Troop at Benacre Denes on land owned by Sir Thomas Gooch. The cost of the two-week camp was five shillings and sixpence (27$^1/_2$p) per Scout, including the rail fare to Lowestoft.

While at this camp they visited the Southwold Boy Scout Rally at Yoxford where they were greatly impressed by the discipline and badges of Sea Scout troops from Cambridge and Southwold. This may have influenced the decision soon after to adopt navy blue as the Troop colour with a uniform of navy blue jersey, shorts and scarves.

Sea Palling
The following year, 1911, a summer camp was held at Sea Palling with Charles Bower as Scout Master. Below is an extract from a diary of this camp written in verse.

One day we smelt an awful stench
It came from out our tent
Thought we, what can it be?
So right inside we went,
When we got in, what do you think
We saw right on the floor?
Young Burrell frying Bloaters fresh
He said: Fresh from the shore

Chief Scout's Rally 1914
By January 1914 the Troop had 17 members and was expanding. By June there were four patrols: Peacocks, Kangaroos, Stags and Otters. Twenty-eight Scouts including Charles Bower and four Assistant Scoutmasters attended the Chief Scout's Rally at Crown Point in Norwich.

Scouts at War: 1914-1918

August 1914: War

Guarding the Telegraph Lines

On the 8th August 1914, soon after war was declared, the County Scout Commissioner received a telegram calling for Scouts to help in the war effort. They were asked to watch the trunk cable lines between Thetford and Bacton in order to prevent them being tapped or cut.

Summer camp, Stratton Strawless, August 1914.

The 1st Norwich Troop was detailed to guard the line from Norwich to Aylsham. Edward Coe tells how

... in an astonishingly short time we were established in camp at Stratton Strawless, which was to be our operational centre. Outwardly, it was an ordinary annual Scout camp but underlying the normal routine was that sense of responsibility. We were part of the organised defences of our Country and although our constant and monotonous patrol duties were onerous we managed to get a certain amount of relaxation in camp.

He recounts how the Scouts carried out their duties conscientiously, collecting hundreds of rounds of live ammunition after an army exercise at the camp and mistakenly capturing a telegraph linesman thought to be tapping the wire.

Coast-watching Duty

Sea Palling

In September, Scouts carried out coast-watching duty for a week at Sea Palling. They worked round the clock in four-hourly shifts recording shipping along the busy coast. Up to 32 vessels including fishing boats, cargo ships and destroyers might be recorded in a typical shift.

The cliff at Mundesley

On December 23rd Charles Bower, with a Sea Scout patrol of seven boys, went to Mundesley for a longer period of duty. They were attached

Coast-watching Patrol, Sea Palling, October 1914. Charles Bower (centre).

to Bacton Coastguard Station and lived in an empty cottage in Mundesley. They watched the coast from the edge of the highest part of the cliffs, three miles from the town.

While on duty they used a tiny shepherd's hut on wheels for shelter. Charles Bower described the hut and their duties.

The hut was about 6 feet by 4 feet, and was awfully cold and draughty on a windy night ... any heavy rain, such as we had most of the time ... came through. (They only had seven nights without rain, hail or snow in the nine and a half weeks they were there.) The cliff was treacherous ... to get to the hut, one had to traverse three-quarters of a mile of cliff path, where there were numerous landslides.

One of the boys, working alone on a rainy night, had a close call when the cliff path he was walking towards fell to the sea.

The shepherd's hut from which the boys watched on the cliff at Mundesley.

The boys worked in pairs, four hours on and eight hours off, night and day, and during the whole period …*there were always one or two wide-awake Scouts on duty.*

They kept a record of all shipping and movement on the coast, reporting immediately anything unusual. The work was hard and monotonous yet the boys worked together as a team … *living out the Scout spirit* which Charles Bower felt was … *testimony to the effect of the Scout Law.*

In their living quarters the patrol did their own cleaning and most of their own catering. They

Coast-watching Scouts, Mundesley, 1914.
Middle row: Norman Dye, Mr A T Nicholls, Charles Bower.

kept the cottage … *like the deck of a man-o'-war … scrubbing the floors once a week, and thoroughly brushing and cleaning the place out twice a day.* Local residents provided them with hot dinners several times a week.

Their hard work and behaviour was such that sceptical local residents entirely changed their previous disapproving opinions of Scouts.

While at Mundesley routine Scouting activities continued. In February 1915 Harold Fildes, with another Scout, completed and recorded a return journey by bicycle to Sea Palling. They passed a mine-sweeper at Happisburgh that had gone ashore the previous September. They saw four destroyers at Sea Palling and met Scouts on duty there who were … *Yorkshire Pit boys.* Fildes commented on how small they were in comparison to the boys from Norfolk. On the way back they saw an aeroplane at Bacton and on arrival at 4.15 pm were … *very tired and not feeling much like going on duty.*

Further duty at Sea Palling
The Patrol went on to do further duty at Sea Palling while still continuing their Scouting activities. By Easter 1915, when all had done at

least three months coast-watching, they were all First Class Scouts.

They worked a roster of two hourly watches around the clock with orderlies appointed to manage general camp duties. There was a Water Orderly, Camp Fatigue Orderlies and Cooks. The Cooks had the task of washing up. In particular, they had to clean out the porringer within two hours of breakfast as well as having to lay the table and brush out the headquarters daily.

A handwritten note on the back of the roster for April 1915 says … *3 funnelled destroyer and 4*

Scouts at the Old Coastguard Station, Sea Palling, 1915.

zeppelins sighted NNE. Believed to be Germans. Wire message to Cromer and Yarmouth at once.

Scouts were given the responsibility for getting all the gear into the lifeboat when it was called out to a vessel in distress. Their ability to achieve this before the crew arrived won them commendation from the County Scoutmaster.

While at Sea Palling the patrol had the honour of an inspection by the Sea Scout Commissioner for London.

Coast-watching in Norfolk
In all, over a hundred Scouts were employed by the Admiralty assisting the Norfolk coastguards. They were stationed at different points on the coast in patrols of around eight boys.

Each Scout was paid seven shillings a week for provisions and pocket money with free medical care available if needed. Accommodation was either rented or given free. If the rooms had a brick or concrete floor, camp beds or bed boards were provided to protect against damp.

Many local residents provided hot meals and

Lady Baden-Powell started a scheme to ensure that all Scouts received a good Christmas Dinner. Prayers were said morning and night, and boys attended religious services on Sundays.

An appeal set up by Lord Albemarle enabled the County Boy Scout Association to provide additional money and clothing. Fuel and light was paid for as well as the cost of boot repairs and new footwear for those who had been on duty for a long period. State insurance was paid and boys who were using their own equipment such as cooking utensils were given a small allowance. Every boy had a warm, blue fisherman's guernsey, and oilskins were available for those on duty.

Hat with 'Coast watching Scout' ribbon, c1915.

The County Scout Master visited fortnightly. He received good reports from the coastguard and the Admiralty on the work of the patrols. The work was considered to be excellent training.

Nearly all lads who have been on any length of time can tell you what class any passing ship belongs to, and they can distinguish the flags of most nations. Above all, the work and need of discipline and self-control is evident to them all day long. (County Scout Master)

Scouts continued coast-watching duties throughout the war and in some cases until 1920. In March 1917, 1st Norwich Scout, N Haughton went on duty at Cley in North Norfolk. He was to continue to do this for two years. Other Scouts did short periods of duty in the summer holidays.

In 1916 six Scouts were awarded the Coast-watching War Service Badge.

Fire service duties
Back at home, junior Scouts helped out at the Fire Station. They worked for long periods out of school hours carrying messages, manning the telephone, cleaning brass and other duties. Most of them gained their Fireman's Badge and at the end of the war were commended by the Chief Constable of Norwich, Mr S A Dain, for carrying out their work with … *celerity, promptitude and willingness.*

Many of the Scouts earned the War Service Badge for one hundred days of service. This included helping out in various ways. Among other things, they raised money at flag days and garden fetes, delivered Red Cross leaflets, collected waste paper and worked at local allotments. They also helped at local hospitals, with convoys of wounded, did air raid duty, helped at Britannia Barracks and provided transport with the trek cart.

100 days of service earned the War Service Badge.

Members of the Troop on Active Service
After the outbreak of war many of the Scouts were eager to join the armed services. Assistant

Coast-watching Scouts, 1915 (first photograph in Sea Scout hats).

Scoutmasters Edward Coe and John Mosby signed up in 1914; Coe as a Lance-Corporal with the 7th Battalion, Norfolk Regiment. He wanted to be a signalman in order to make use of his six years experience in the Boy Scouts. He later said the experience … *proved its worth and a second stripe soon adorned my sleeves.* He was to go on and win the Military Cross in 1918.

Three years later John Mosby had become an Observer with the Royal Flying Corps. He was awarded the Distinguished Service Order in

1st Norwich Sea Scouts with the Trek Cart.
It was used to provide transport as part of their war service
(All were First Class Scouts and four were King's Scouts).

1918. After his pilot had been killed in an attack by three enemy planes, although wounded twice in the abdomen, he managed to right the plane and land safely.

In November 1915 Scout Master Charles Bower joined the 16th Sherwood Foresters. In April 1916 Patrol Leader Norman Dye joined up, followed in 1917 by Assistant Scout Master Middleton. By October 1917 all the officers of the Scout Troop were on active service.

Mr A.T. Nicholls, Honorary Scoutmaster
Mr Arthur T Nicholls had first taken an interest in the Troop in 1912 and was their President in December 1914 when he was given the title of Honorary Scout Master. He later took over the running of the Troop for the duration of the war. On leaving for France in April 1916, Charles Bower wrote to thank him for stepping in just when they were wondering if they could keep the Troop going.

Charles Bower killed in action
On September 13th 1917 Charles Bower was killed in action. The Troop, devastated at the news, expressed their deepest sympathy to his parents and fiancée. A moving memorial service at St Thomas' Church impressed upon them the example he had set for them to follow.

Edward Coe was invited to take over as Scout Master. He accepted the position expressing a hope that he could carry on in the same spirit as Charles Bower, working to make the 1st Norwich the best in the country.

Roll of Honour
Fifty 1st Norwich Scouts served in the armed forces during the war. Twelve of them lost their lives including A.C. Pearce, who had won the Military Cross in 1917. A memorial service for all Norwich Scouts killed during the war was held at St Andrew's Hall. Thirty 1st Norwich Scouts attended and words written by Charles Bower from the front, were read during the service.

Roll of Honour 1914-1918

C F Bower, Scout Master

N E E Burton-Fanning

N S Dye, Assistant Scout Master

C D M Fowler

L S Glover, Patrol Leader

A G Gibling

A C Pearce, MC

R Spicer

H Thorn

C Thouless

N B Bavin

R Vince

Captain Bower's Own

Scout Master Charles Bower, c1915.

Norman Dye, 1914.

Edward Coe was appointed Scout Master after the death of Charles Bower in 1917 while he was still a serving officer. He did not take over the day-to-day running of the Troop until June 1919. Mr Nicholls, who had been Honorary Scout Master since December 1914, was presented with a pair of field glasses in acknowledgement of the work he had done during the difficult years of the war.

The Troop made a fresh start with several changes. In honour of their fallen Scout Master they took on the new title of 1st Norwich Boy Scouts (Captain Bower's Own). In memory of Scout Norman Dye, his favourite expression 'It Can Be Done' was adopted as the Troop motto and embroidered on the uniform neckerchief.

The patrols were reorganised and it was decided to follow the 'Indian Scheme' along the lines of that started some years earlier by Mr E Thompson Seton, who later became the Chief Scout of America. It put an emphasis on woodcraft, courage, common sense and self-control. The Scouts adopted Native American names, and feathers were awarded as marks of achievement. A concert was given soon after, where Scouts performed items based on the Scheme in order to explain it to parents.

In 1919, the first Rover Patrol was formed for Scouts over sixteen years of age. With eight Rovers and six warranted officers, the Troop now had a total membership of forty-nine.

In the spring of 1921, a Wolf Cub Pack was started with ten 8 to 11 year old boys. Miss Mary Easton, who had been the fiancée of Charles Bower, became the lady Cub Master with Alfred Palmer as her Assistant. A year later Harvey Watling became the first Cub to move up to the Scout Troop.

The expanded Troop continued throughout the 1920s with a full programme of meetings and events. Pioneering and camping were main activities along with swimming, concerts, community service and badge work. Overnight

1st Norwich Indian Display at the Association Rally, Crown Point, 1919.

and weekend camps were held as well as a long summer camp each year.

Several notable Norfolk landowners, who were involved in the Scout Movement at the time, gave permission for Scouts to camp on their estates. Among the campsites used by the 1st Norwich were those at Benacre, Taverham, Quidenham,

The Troop at Earlham House, 1922. Left to right, middle row: 4th left, J Mosby, Mrs Coe, E Coe, Mr G Bower, Miss Easton. Centre front: Scout N Coe.

Costessey, Happisburgh and Eccles.

The Troop also took part in District and Association Rallies and sent representatives to the World Jamborees.

Many activities took the form of competition, which was considered to be a great incentive to learning and efficiency. Awards and trophies were given for achievement in different areas of endeavour, often for teamwork.

Neville Coe

Neville Coe, who was later to become Cub Master, was the younger brother of Scout Master Edward Coe. He received the Cornwell Award (the Scout Badge of Courage) in 1920. This was in recognition of the courage and fortitude he had demonstrated after suffering a serious burn while cooking at camp. His patrol was in the running to win a camping competition and in order not to let the other Scouts down, he kept quiet about his injury, enduring great pain for many hours until it was discovered.

In 1922 he was the first in the county to gain the Bushman's Thong (Ranger Cord). To qualify for this he would have completed his First Class and Venturer Badges plus two others chosen from: Camp Warden, Forester, Naturalist, Meteorologist, Pioneer, Tracker and Astronomer. In the same year he went climbing in the Alps with Asst. Scout Master Middleton.

Years later, during the Second World War he again demonstrated courage and presence of mind. On arriving at Headquarters with two Scouts, and on hearing the air raid siren and the drone of a V1 rocket, he threw the Scouts to the ground, spreading his own body on top to protect them. David Baxter, lying face-up underneath, saw the rocket pass overhead and heard the explosion as it crashed two miles away. All three then got up and carried on as normal.

Patrol Competition

Regular Patrol competitions had been held since 1916 when Scouts were examined individually on general knowledge of the Scout Movement and practical things such as how to set up camp. Percentage marks were awarded and the Patrol with the highest aggregate score won the Patrol Shield to keep in their den. (In January 1919 when Stanley Clarke achieved the highest mark of 94.3%, Edward Coe saw fit to write a congratulatory letter to inform his parents.)

Miss Easton presented a set of antlers to the Troop in 1920. They were awarded every three months to the Patrol earning the most marks for gaining Proficiency Badges and completing parts of their

Cub Master Neville Coe (back row, left) with Cub Pack. c1932.

Second Class Badge. From 1924, First Class Badges and King's Scout Awards also counted in the competition. As well as keeping the Antlers for three months, the winning patrol was allowed to use the Rovers' Den, was put in charge of the Troop Colours at Church Parades, and the Patrol Leader became Chairman of the Court of Honour. Thirty years on, the award had changed and from the 1950s until the 1980s the best Patrol received a Leopard's Head trophy, with the Antlers awarded to the Patrol with the smartest uniform.

The Antlers, presented to the Troop by Miss Easton in 1920.

Owl Patrol, winners of the County Camping Trophy at Mousehold Aerodrome, 1926.

Camping Competitions

The Camp Shield was won by the Patrol recording the greatest number of camping nights per member.

The Camping Trophy was presented to the Troop in 1923. The competition to win it included elements such as attendance at bathing parades and personal hygiene while at camp. At the end of Summer Camp, marks for the year were aggregated and the trophy awarded.

The Camping Trophy.

Chief Scout, Sir Robert Baden-Powell presents the Otter Shield, 1926.

Swimming

Every Scout in the Troop was expected to learn to swim and many went on to gain Royal Life Saving Society awards, including the Bronze Medallion. Individual swimming records were posted on a board at Headquarters and a trophy was given to the best Patrol.

In the early days they used the Swan Baths in Heigham Street where the pool was heated by the boilers of the attached laundry. Mr Ransome, the proprietor, taught the boys to swim by shouting instructions as he hauled them along the pool, using a pole attached to a rope looped around their chests. Later they swam in the outdoor baths at Lakenham and from 1934 at the Lido Swimming Pool.

The Otter Shield.

The Troop won the Otter Challenge Shield in 1921 and again in 1925. This was a national swimming award given each year to the Troop with the highest percentage of boys who had learnt to swim, also taking into account other swimming and life-saving badges they had gained.

Annual Swimming Sports were held which developed into spectacular Swimming Galas. The bottom of the pool was illuminated for the displays which included acts such as diving head first through a ring of fire. There was a popular inter-troop relay and later, events were opened to other Swimming Clubs such as the Penguins, the Swan Club and the Lads' Club.

A Troop Swimming Club was formed in 1927 and affiliated to the Midland District Amateur Swimming Association and the Royal Life Saving Society. It was later affiliated to the Norfolk County Amateur Swimming Association, established in1929. The Group organised their last Swimming Sports in 1935, handing over to the Penguins Swimming Club, to whom they also gave the team diving trophy.

District and National Competitions
The Troop was successful in District and National competitions throughout the 1920s.

In the years 1925, 1926 and 1927 the Troop won the Norfolk County Camping Competition and were awarded the Albemarle Camping Trophy. In 1926, they were honoured to receive both the Otter Shield and the Camping Trophy from the Chief Scout, Sir Robert Baden-Powell at the Norfolk County Rally held at Mousehold Aerodrome.

The War Canoe

The War Canoe

In spite of general opinion that it was too ambitious a project, in the winter of 1924 the Troop began to build a twenty-eight foot canoe made of wood and covered with canvas. It was five and a half feet wide with a high curved prow built to carry fourteen paddlers and eight passengers. It was built in the Swan Baths on Heigham Street, with support from the proprietor Mr Keymer, who was later presented with a Thanks badge, and a local boat-builder who loaned a steam box for bending the wood.

The keel was made of 2" ash and the ribs of 2" x 3/8" American rock elm. The outer canvas was stretched tightly over closely fitted 1/4" boards and coated with linseed oil to make it tight and smooth. It was finished with two coats of undercoat and one of enamel and fitted with an ash gunwhale.

The War Canoe built in dry dock at Swan Baths, Heigham St. Norwich, c1924.

The launching of the canoe made headlines locally and was mentioned in the national press. It was used for fifteen years on the Norfolk Broads and rivers. *It never turned over or sank but passed peacefully away during the last war.* (Skipper Coe, Memoirs)

Chief Scout, Sir Robert Baden-Powell, travels in the War Canoe from Thorpe Station to Pulls Ferry, 1926.

The Troop motto 'It can be done' was painted on the prow of the canoe which later came to be called Peewit I.

In 1926, on the occasion of the Norwich Rally, the Chief Scout, Sir Robert Baden-Powell was taken as a passenger in the canoe from Foundry Bridge near Thorpe Station to Pull's Ferry, where he was to inspect the Norwich Troops by the Nelson Monument.

With a full quota on Wroxham Broad, 1928.

Trying to negotiate under the girder at Drayton.

Sea Scouts

A new Patrol: Seagulls 1926
After their success with the War Canoe, the Troop decided to re-form a patrol of Sea Scouts, the original Patrol having lapsed after the First World War. In November 1926 members of the Senior patrol became Sea Scouts and changed their patrol name from Owls to Seagulls. Younger members of the Troop who … *couldn't wait to be Seniors* were disappointed that they had to retain their … *big hats* and remain Boy Scouts. (Alfred Buttle, 'Sandy')

'Peewit' on Wroxham Broad.

Edward Coe, Group Scoutmaster 1928-1947
From the early days of Scouting, Troops were registered with the Secretary of their local District Association, and from 1919 a register was held nationally at Imperial Headquarters of the Boy Scouts Association in London.

In 1928 all Troops were required to re-register with the London Headquarters under a new Group System which recorded all the different sections - Wolf Cubs, Scouts and Rovers. The 1st Norwich Group (Capt. Bower's Own) duly registered under the Norwich South District of the Norfolk County Boy Scouts Association.

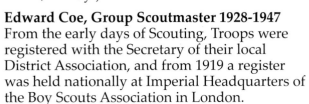
Group Registration Document, 1928.

Edward Coe now became Group Scout Master as well as Scout Master. There were seven other warranted Leaders at the time: four Assistant Scout Masters, an Acting Rover Leader, Cub Master and Acting Cub Master. The fifty-three other Group members consisted of twenty-four Scouts, six Sea Scouts, twelve Wolf Cubs, six Rover Scouts and five Rover Sea Scouts.

Enthusiasm for water activities continued to grow especially after the Troop was given use of a waterside base and boats at Wroxham Broad. The 1st Norwich Group continued to prosper and gain in reputation culminating in an invitation for the Sea Scouts to represent Great Britain at the first International Sea Scout Jamboree in Poland in 1932. A contingent of thirteen Scouts and Rovers travelled to Poland, coming second in the overall competition after being narrowly beaten by Hungary.

Juniors become Sea Scouts
In 1935, after moving to new Headquarters on the river at Old Lakenham Hall, it was decided that all the Scouts would become Sea Scouts, a decision very popular with the juniors. Patrols now had responsibility for keeping and maintaining their own canoes. Scouts could take the boats out with permission from the Patrol Leader but they had to be in uniform when on the water. Those who could swim sometimes took boats out on overnight journeys.

The Senior Patrol had most freedom and spent much time at their headquarters on Wroxham Broad. In 1938 a second Senior Patrol, Owls, was formed and two boats were repaired for them to take over.

Sea Scouts were awarded white tops to wear on their black hats only when they had gained their 2nd Class Badge and passed a 50 yards swimming test. An exception was made in 1944 when a Scout whose health prohibited him from swimming was awarded his white hat after passing his Handyman's badge. That same year the junior Scouts were also allowed to wear 'white tops', but just for the summer. It was not until the 1950s that white hats were worn all the time.

Sea Scouts at Wroxham 1926-1936
In 1926 the Troop had been given use of a boathouse at the top end of Wroxham Broad, known as the 'pond'. They were to use this as Sea Scout headquarters until it was sold and closed down in 1936. Here the Sea Scouts and Rovers spent considerable time, often cycling and sometimes walking from Norwich to Wroxham to stay overnight. (On one occasion two Scouts walked there and back on a cold Christmas morning, arriving home in time for dinner with their families.) Some of the best times they had were when they cycled

Canoeing on the 'Pond' at Wroxham Broad. To the left of centre is the entrance to the Broad.

Ex-Scouts have recalled happy times sailing, rowing, canoeing and swimming on the Broads and rivers, sometimes doing overnight journeys or longer trips by boat. There is a story of Skipper Coe sailing a half-decker across the bows of a rather smart Norfolk One Design and whipping the helmsman out ... *neatly as you please* leaving him trailing in the water hanging on to the half-decker's creaking bowsprit. (T. Killick, 'Chuck')

In 1930, the Chief Scout, Sir Robert Baden-Powell and His Royal Highness Prince George both visited the boathouse. In the same year, the Sea Scouts gave a display at Wroxham Regatta, which included diving from the flying boat and an obstacle dinghy racing. It was well received and they were invited to give a repeat performance the following year.

The crow's nest, high above Sea Scout HQ.

Sea Scout HQ at Wroxham Broad, 1935.

over in winter and ... *played records after dark with a huge jug of coffee near the fire.* (Mr A E Batch,'Shrimp')

The Headquarters provided a base for water activities and somewhere to stay. Over time they acquired several boats as well as the War Canoe, including two old wherries and two flying boats. They worked maintaining and waterproofing the boats and improving the site, using practical skills acquired through Scouting. A flag-staff with crow's nest was erected, and a gateway was constructed as well as a bridge over the dyke.

A rowing four, c1932.

23

*View from the crow's nest
(Scouts having lunch, bottom right), 1929.*

Slithy & Seagull on Wroxham Broad, 1929.

Edward Coe, Group Scoutmaster from 1928 to 1947

Edward 'Skipper' Coe was an outstanding Scout Leader who devoted a large part of his life to the Scout Movement.

His Scouting career began in 1908 when, at the age of thirteen, he and Lawrence Glover started Lion Patrol, which became the foundation

Edward Coe, 1922.

of the 1st Norwich Sea Scout Group. His enthusiasm was such that he soon became a First Class Scout and had gained his King's Scout Badge by 1910.

During the First World War he served in the Army attaining the rank of Captain and winning the Military Cross. He was appointed Scout Master in 1917 and became Group Scoutmaster in 1928, a position he held until 1947 when he became President of the Group.

He took on the additional role of District Scout Master in 1919 and later served for nine years as Deputy County Commissioner. On his retirement in 1952, in recognition of his service to Scouting, he was made County Vice-President and honorary Deputy Camp Chief at Gilwell Park. In 1959 he became a founder member of the First Norwich Group of Old Scouts (FINGOS).

Under his leadership, particularly in the 1920s and 1930s, the Scout Group expanded and flourished, to include Wolf Cubs, Rover Scouts and Sea Scouts, all undertaking a great variety of activities. In 1929 he was awarded the Silver Wolf and in 1932 he led the 1st Norwich Sea Scout Patrol representing Great Britain at the first International Sea Scout Jamboree in Poland.

As a memorial, after his death in 1964, FINGOS presented the Group with furniture for the Court of Honour and set up a small camp Chapel in the grounds of Old Lakenham Hall. Later a larger outdoor Chapel was built in his memory at County Scout Association Headquarters at Eaton Vale, Norwich.

Wherries

There were reportedly two old wherries moored at the Headquarters; one called the Silver Cloud.

The Scouts worked hard to keep them afloat. They scraped the black rotten wood from the bottom of one wherry prior to concreting it, managing to keep it afloat for more than a season before it sank.

Trying to dry dock the wherry, 1935.

Getting the wherry into dry dock proved to be a hopeless endeavour.

The F5 flying boat hull and wherry at Wroxham, 1935.

The Flying Boats

In 1930 the Scouts acquired the hull of a 1918, F5 flying boat, which they transported by lorry from Mousehold Aerodrome to a yacht station near Wroxham bridge. It was launched and towed by the War Canoe to the Headquarters on the Broad where they planned to use it to provide extra sleeping accommodation.

The hull was painted, the inside renovated and a diving platform built on the back. With an outboard motor fitted and the steering gear fixed up, the flying boat was used to make journeys on the river although the unreliability of the motor meant that it

Scouts in the war canoe towing the F5 flying boat to their HQ on Wroxham Broad, 1930.

sometimes had to be towed back by canoe. It was used for displays on Wroxham Broad and at the Jamboree on Salhouse Broad in 1930.

A second flying boat (N4934) was acquired in 1935 and again transported by lorry to Wroxham bridge and launched. This time a dinghy with an outboard motor was used to tow it to Headquarters.

An engine and propeller were duly mounted on the front. However, swinging the propeller to start the engine gave Scouts sore fingers and once it was going they became covered in oily exhaust smuts. The plane was only able to go with the wind so a lot of paddling was needed to avoid collisions. (A E Batch, 'Shrimp')

Preparing the flying boat N4934 to be taken to Wroxham, 1935.

Flying boat N4934 moored at HQ, 1935.

Flying boat N4934 showing the propeller, 1935.

Diving from flying boat N4934. Wroxham, 1935.

Poland 1932

The First International Sea Scout Jamboree
The 1st Norwich Sea Scouts were invited by the Boy Scouts Association to represent Great Britain at the first International Sea and Water Scout Jamboree held at Garczyn in Poland in August 1932. The Jamboree took the form of a competition with a number of different events

The International Patrol with Skipper Coe, seated centre.

The International Patrol. Poland 1932	
Leader Edward H Coe (Skipper)	
Rover Sea Scouts	
Mate	J A Watling (Toby)
Second	J H Braybrooks (Tadpole)
	T W Killick (Chuckle)
	D J Rabson (Rabbits)
	D W Brown (Sambo)
	G G Martin (Zip)
	M A Rabson (Wilfred)
	G Simmen (Felix)
	Clarke (Squeak)
Sea Scouts	
	H G Hanson (Pip)
	A M Abel (Yabo)
Patrol Leader	S C Braybrooks (Brawny)

including: sailing, boat-pulling, swimming, diving, life-saving, canoe management, sail repairing, knotting and splicing, first aid, rope and life-buoy throwing, signalling using semaphore, morse and international flag codes, and a 15 minute camp fire entertainment.

Other competing countries were Czechoslovakia, France, Hungary, Latvia and Rumania. The Polish Scouts did not compete but acted as hosts and gave displays of water activities.

As soon as they had agreed to go, the Troop formed an International Patrol of twelve Scouts and Rover Scouts. With Skipper Coe as Leader they began training in March. Meeting at least twice a week and at weekends, they received sailing tuition from members of the Yacht Club at Wroxham Broad as well as instruction in boat pulling from the Lord Nelson Training Ship at Riverside in Norwich. Mr Hales, a sail-maker, taught them how to splice ropes and make sail repairs, and a naval Officer helped them learn to signal using international code flags. They practised life-saving skills at the Swan Swimming Club and put together a programme of mouth organ pieces for the camp-fire entertainment.

All members of the Patrol managed to gain permission to attend the Jamboree, a few having to negotiate leave of absence from somewhat reluctant employers. The journey was arranged by Cook's Travel Agency at a cost of £8 a head with accommodation and meals provided on the way. Each Scout carried his own kit, including a new

At Berlin Aerodrome.

sheath knife and a specially designed hike tent that could be erected using a thumbstick as the pole.

Travelling by train, they camped overnight at Gilwell Park, slept in a church hall as guests

Hike tents with thumbsticks as poles.

Gateway to 1st Norwich camp, depicting their motto 'It Can Be Done'.

of the British Scouts in Brussels, and stayed in a hotel in Cologne. In Berlin each Scout was given home hospitality by a German Scout. They were taken sight-seeing, then welcomed by the German Air Minister and given an aeroplane flight over the city, a new experience for most of them. Later they were entertained with dinner at the Foreign Students Club where they had to sit through a long political speech about the Polish Corridor.

After an uncomfortable overnight journey, they were met at Chojnice, on the Polish border by an interpreter (who was soon replaced for not being up to the job), and a Polish Scout Master, whose uniform they were surprised to note included a peaked cap, axe and Browning automatic gun. Here they boarded a train for the Jamboree site.

It was pulled by an old locomotive that was so slow, some of the Scouts were able to climb up and travel on the roof and one even got down and ran alongside.

Second place in the boat-pulling.

On arrival they were greeted by an official reception at the station. They didn't understand a word that was said, but Skipper Coe nevertheless made a short speech in reply. A band played God Save the King and around two thousand cheering Polish Scouts lined the short route to the camp. At the camp they were taken to the central flag-staff where the Polish flag was hauled down and the Red Ensign attached below it. Once again the band struck up God Save the King.

The Scouts refused the large tents with bedsteads and straw mattresses offered to them and, to the bemusement of the Poles, set about putting up their small hike tents. They then erected a gateway before having a meal and joining the camp-fire.

The camp was by a large lake surrounded by pine forest. On the lake the

Prizes won in the competition.

Polish Army had erected landing stages, diving platforms, a swimming enclosure and a seventy-foot observation tower, mainly for use by the judges. Most of the events were held here but there was also sailing on a lake near Chojnice, and the boat tug-of-war at a place called Hel at Gdynia.

A ceremony was held two days later on August 7th when the Chief Scout's representative, Mr Hubert Martin, the International Commissioner for Scouting, arrived. There then followed eight days of intense competition in which the team from Great Britain did well.

They won the kayak race and the overnight kayak excursion, which involved travelling five miles by night, making camp and reporting back exactly twelve hours after departure. They won the international sailing competition with much acclaim and won every heat and the final in the boat tug of war. (Although smaller than their opponents, they beat them by rowing in perfect time and using short strokes.)

They came second in the boat-pulling with obstacles and the individual contests such as rope throwing, kayak sailing, lifesaving, plate diving, first aid, splicing, boat repairing, and sewing a sail. They also came second in the swimming competition, which included diving, life-saving and making a raft.

In the overall competition they finished second, seven points behind Hungary. They were awarded an ornate brass clock, which they brought home along with a selection of other prizes and souvenirs including a Rob Roy canoe.

While in Poland the Scouts made excursions to Torun, Posnan and Gdynia where they were shown the sights, given banquets and listened to speeches they usually couldn't understand. They expressed great admiration for the Polish Scouts and their hospitality and struck up a lasting friendship with Teddy Wolski, their second interpreter. He was an American-born Pole and was to visit the Scouts in England a year later.

Skipper Coe writes of the varied impressions they had of Poland at the time. They saw … *extreme poverty, patriotism equal to our own, simple living, and a feeling that the whole country was recovering from a knock-out blow.* The two-hour closing ceremony was somewhat of an ordeal with … *speeches, march-pasts* and … *an orgy of saluting and hand-shaking.* Then, when they were trying to pack up camp they were beleaguered with autograph hunters and Scouts wanting to swap badges. Nevertheless, Skipper Coe was proud of the Troop's achievements and felt that they had … *upheld the best traditions of our seafaring nation.*

The journey home was not uneventful. Due to a misunderstanding they missed the train and spent the first night sleeping in an empty railway car in a siding near the camp site. Later, they left a bundle of souvenir walking sticks on the train in Norwich. These, luckily, were found the next day in Sheringham and returned.

On return they received the following message from the Chief Scout:

> *Well Done! Norwich, for the good Scouting you showed at the Polish International Jamboree.*
>
> *You Rover Scouts! May you have every success in the Quests you are working out for happifying yourselves and other people.*
>
> Baden-Powell of Gilwell

The Second World War

Capt. Coe heads a Parade of the Home Guard in Tombland, including several 1st Norwich Rover Scouts.

During the Second World War Scouts were once again given useful and responsible tasks to perform. They provided messenger services, particularly for the Home Guard, sometimes having to travel over fields and unmade roads in the dark. They also helped with Air Raid Patrols, and performed other civic duties including waste paper collection, which earned them both congratulations and thanks from the Local Authority. At the County camp at Holkham in 1945 the Troop was responsible for telephone line communication to the Coast Guard lookout.

One of the jobs the Scouts were given during the Blitz, was to carry water in a galvanised bath from a well in Old Lakenham to a Rest Centre at the school on Smithfield Road. Carl Buttle remembered having very wet shoes and socks, and not much water in the bath, after carrying it up Long John Hill.

Activities of the Group continued during the war although there were few Leaders available and Scout numbers dropped. In 1943 numbers were so low they had to carry on without Patrols for a time. Some new members were recruited however, and in 1944 there were two Patrols, Stags and Kangaroos. Alan Baxter (Baccy) transferred from another Group during this time, to save travelling. He was persuaded to join when Scouts came to his house to erect a Morrison shelter. He became a Patrol Leader, Senior Patrol Leader and later took over from Neville Coe as Cub Master.

Peter Martin (Cox'un) led the Troop for a year before becoming Scout Master in 1944. He was called up for a second time in 1945 leaving two Assistant Scout Masters to take charge for a time until Alfred Buttle (Sandy, also nicknamed Parrot) took over.

Alfred Buttle had been in the services and earned the DSM. He remained in Scouting and was later awarded the Silver Wolf and honoured with an MBE. Many other Scouts also served during the war: Percy Beak (Peak) went into the Dragoon Guards, Basil Craske (Nuts) became a bomber pilot, was shot down and made a Prisoner of War, Henry Todd (Toddles) who had played a major part in building the 1st Norwich Headquarters at Old Lakenham Hall, went into the Royal Air Force and was later reported missing.

At one time there were twenty-seven 1st Norwich Rover Scouts and Leaders serving in His Majesty's Forces. Sadly, as in the First World War, some of the Scouts lost their lives.

Roll of Honour

1939-1945

H Adair

J R Braybrooks

S C Braybrooks

H Todd

Skipper Greenfield Takes Over

The Second World War took its toll on the 1st Norwich Group and by the winter of 1946 finances were low, boats and equipment had deteriorated, and there were only enough Scouts to form one Patrol. As things began to improve in 1947 changes were made to the leadership. Eric Greenfield was appointed Scout Master and

Mr. A. J. (John) Seymour took on the role of Group Scout Master, a position he held for the next three years before handing it on to Skipper Eric Greenfield in 1950. Edward Coe retired and became President of the Group. Membership soon rose back up to thirty Scouts and eighteen Rovers.

Eric Greenfield's father-in-law, Mr W C Young of Letchworth, gave the Scouts use of some land, a building and a private dyke at 'Sunray' on Wroxham Broad. This became their new Sea Scout headquarters and was officially opened in 1948 by the County Commissioner, Col. H J Cator, a former 1st Norwich Rover who was affectionately known as Ratty.

Skipper Greenfield at St George's Day, 1958.

The facility on the Broad enabled the Scouts to camp and undertake water activities that could not be carried

out on the river at Old Lakenham. They had several boats including a Wishbone dinghy, six kayaks and a three-quarter decker sailing boat, the Zephyr. David Baxter has memories of the converted railway carriage on site, where they met to … *sing songs and do individual turns.* He remembers the Zephyr … *which was so fast it terrified us.* He tells, in turn, of terrifying the local fishermen when sailing Skipper's sea-going yacht with no adult supervision, often misjudging the turn and taking their fishing rods

On the water at Wroxham Sea Scout headquarters c1950.

trailing behind the boat.

The Scouts enjoyed these headquarters on the Broad until 1955, when Mr Young died and it was sold. In September of that year the boats were moved to Decoy Broad at Woodbastwick, which was to become the main base for 1st Norwich water activities. Here, the Scouts built themselves a wooden hut for boat storage and occasional accommodation. In the early 1960s, Scouts taking the hut down to replace it, found 'pin-ups' hidden behind the wall panelling. It is rumoured that the same pin-ups were brought back to Norwich and relocated behind panelling at Scout Headquarters where they remain to this day.

Regular camps were held at Decoy Broad and there are stories of some unofficial camping in the 1950s, in particular, during one winter when the boys concerned were afraid of being discovered because of the tell-tale tracks they left in the snow.

Skipper Greenfield was Group Scout Master for twenty-three years from 1950 to 1973, during which time there was a full and active membership. The Group expanded in spite of a continued shortage of leaders in the early 1950s when several of the older members were still away on National Service. Towards the end of the decade there were sixty-two Group members.

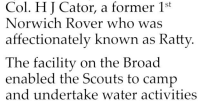

Skipper Greenfield (second left) with fellow Leaders from Holland, Nigeria, France and Germany, 1959.

Eric Greenfield Group Scout Master 1950-1973

Skipper Greenfield receiving the Silver Acorn Medal, August 1976.

Nicknamed 'Twink' as a young Cub, Eric Greenfield moved through the ranks as Cub Sixer, Scout Patrol Leader and Troop Leader, to become Scout Master in 1947 when he was given the new title of 'Skipper'. He took over as Group Scout Master in 1950 and held the position until 1973.

He was Norwich South District Commissioner from 1960 to 1976 and Assistant County Commissioner (Norwich) from 1976 to 1983.

Cutting the 70th Anniversary cake, 1978.

Always an active and dedicated Scout he represented the Troop at the World Scout Jamboree in Holland in 1937 and was responsible for the long-standing partnership with the Hohenlimburg Troop in Germany.

Under his leadership all sections of the Troop enjoyed a full programme of activities, both land-based and on the water.

He was rewarded for his services to Scouting with the Medal of Merit in 1959 and the Silver Acorn in 1976.

Left: Eric Greenfield (Twink), front, as a young Cub with 'Pip' Hanson. c1933.

Right:Eric Greenfield's Scout badges, including his King's Scout Badge (top, centre).

As well as the usual outdoor activities and badge work, the Group gained several distinctions and took part in local and international jamborees and regattas. A long-lasting friendship was made with the Hohenlimburg Troop in Germany and several exchange visits took place.

In 1956 when funds were low, a group of five Scouts hiked to the Jamboree at Sandringham, pulling a trek cart and taking two days to get there. The programme for 1958 included a Regatta, an Open Night, a Whitsun camp at Woodbastwick, a Square Dance, a Jamboree, and a Fathers' Night. The Cub section was particularly strong with Cubs taking part in many activities, giving concerts and going on Pack holidays. A parents committee was set

On the journey from Norwich to Sandringham, using the trek cart, August 1956. Left to right: Brian Hunn, Julian O'Dell, ? Tye, Brian Buxton.

up to help with fundraising. Fetes, bingo and other events were regularly held and a new Headquarters was built and opened in 1967.

Admiralty Recognition
In 1952 the 1st Norwich were the first Sea Scouts in Norfolk to achieve Admiralty Recognition. This entitled them to wear a special badge and to fly an Ensign defaced with a crown and the Scout badge. It also gave them access to the loan of equipment from the Admiralty and the chance for Scouts to go aboard Royal Navy ships. Further annual inspections by a Royal Navy officer saw the continuation of recognition for several years.

The Norfolk Truck
The Scouts won the HMS Norfolk Truck in 1953 for making best progress during the year. The Truck (a naval term for the top of a flagstaff) was made from brass shell cases used by the RN

County-class heavy cruiser during the Second World War. It took the form of a naval crown with a Scout badge in the centre, on which is

The colour party after being presented with the Norfolk Truck, St George's Day 1953. Left to right: Scout Lenny Aldridge, Senior Scout John Webster, Cub?.

enamelled the crest of the ship. Among her exploits during the war, HMS Norfolk played a part in the sinking of the Bismarck in 1941. She was scrapped in 1953.

Coronation Year 1953
In 1953, the year of the coronation of Queen Elizabeth II, Scouts attended the three-day Jamboree at Sandringham with Cubs and

Boiling water thirty feet up a tree, early 1950's. 'Bunny' High on the right

John Grimmer, the first winner of the Cockle Trophy, 1958.

The Cockle Trophy, presented to the Group by Mr & Mrs Hunn in memory of their son Brian, nicknamed Cockle.

parents visiting on the last day. On the day of the Coronation, 2nd June 1953, Scouts around the country lit a chain of beacons to celebrate. Skipper Greenfield and another District Scout Master were in charge of the beacon on St James Hill in Norwich. Scouts from the 1st, 22nd and 29th Norwich Troops built the fire using eight lorry-loads of wood. It was twenty feet in diameter, twenty feet high and fuelled by fourteen gallons of oil. A crowd of several hundred watched and shouted 'God Save the Queen' as the fire was lit to a Royal salute of two rockets. (Untitled press cutting)

District Camping Competition

The Troop won the District Senior Camping Competition in the early 1950s at Rackheath. The Competition took the form of a journey (by bicycle) to a map reference, with obstacles to overcome en route, an overnight camp and return. There is a record of boys completing a test at around this time where, in case of flood, they had to light a fire and boil water within twenty minutes, while up a tree, thirty feet above the ground.

The Cockle Trophy

The Cockle Trophy was awarded every six months to a junior Scout for individual achievement. It was presented to the Group in 1957 by the parents of Brian Hunn, nicknamed 'Cockle', who had tragically taken his own life. Scout John Grimmer was proud to be the first to receive it and he went on to hold it for twelve months.

W. Fischer and C. Green, winners of the Tillett Cup for the All-comers event, Decoy Regatta, 1969.

Skipper Greenfield is presented with leaving gifts, 1973.

Continued Success

In the 1960s and 70s Scouts had success in many competitions. They came first in the Norwich South First Aid competition in 1961, Hawks won the mini-Olympics in 1968, and in the same year, the Fischer brothers won the Bronze Scout Award for Skiing. They also enjoyed success on the water. They took first place at the Decoy Regatta in 1969 and the next year won the Tillett Cup for the All Comers Event. In 1970 they won five trophies at the National Scout Regatta at Birmingham, including the Cannon Ball Trophy for Dinghy pulling (under 16 feet) and, in 1972, they gained first place in the single Kayak competition at Wensum Regatta.

A Long Lasting Friendship - The Hohenlimburg Troop Germany

In 1953 two Scouts from Hohenlimburg in Germany came to Norwich and went with the 1st Norwich Scouts to the Coronation Jamboree at Sandringham. One of them, Gustav Stefan, was made an Honorary Member of the Troop and the meeting proved to be the beginning of a long-lasting, international friendship.

In 1957, three German Scouts, en route to the 9th World Jamboree at Sutton Coldfield, stayed in Norwich with Skipper Greenfield. They were invited to attend the 1st Norwich Group's, 50th Anniversary celebrations the following year, and a larger party of fifteen came.

At the Coronation Jamboree, Sandringham, 1953.
Left to right: Basil Craske, Hans Olock, Eric Greenfield, Gustav Stefan, Frank Folkard.

German Scouts at the 1st Norwich 50th Anniversary Dinner, 1958.

In 1959, eighteen 1st Norwich Scouts with Skipper Greenfield and two other leaders made a visit to Germany. They stayed for eight days in the homes of Hohenlimburg Scouts and spent a week in a Scout House in the mountains. They took with them greetings from the Lord Mayor of Norwich to the Burgermeister of Hohenlimburg along with the hope that the visit … *would further cement the bond of friendship between our two people, especially those of the Scouts.*

In 1961 a party of twenty-five German Scouts (including one girl, who was Akela of the Cub

Skipper Greenfield presenting a letter to the Burgermeister of Hohenlimburg from the Lord Mayor of Norwich, 1959.

Pack) came to Norwich for a fortnight under the leadership of Mr Waldo Patzer. The first week was spent at a Jamboree at Taverham Mill with English and French Scouts and the second at the homes of 1st Norwich Scouts. In the same year Alan Adcock and John Curtis made a visit to Germany.

In 1963, Skipper Greenfield with seven Scouts travelled by car to a week-long camp beside a lake at Listertalsperre. They visited Hohenlimburg en route, staying with the German Scouts. Three of the seven and one other returned in 1965, staying in a Youth Hostel. They took with them the gift of an English

Scouts at Thorpe Station leaving for Germany, 1959. Leaders: Centre back, Basil Craske (Nuts). Extreme right, Skipper Eric Greenfield standing next to James White (Pilot).

Oak tree to be planted in a new park called Lennepark. They also took a tape-recording made by Skipper Greenfield in which he talked about the significance of the gift marking twelve years of friendship between the two Scout Troops. The Scouts went on to a camp and then stayed at the homes of German Scouts at Bergnestadt before returning to Norwich.

A further visit to Germany was made in 1966 and the German Scouts came to Norwich in 1968.

In 1969 Norwich Scouts went to Hohenlimburg again carrying further messages between the Lord Mayor and Burgermeister. A ceremony was held in the Lennepark at the oak planted four years earlier. A plaque commemorating the event was placed under the tree and

Alan Adcock (left) & John Curtis with a German friend, 1961.

Five years later in 1974, another visit was paid to Norwich by the German Scouts and, in 1975, twenty 1st Norwich Scouts visited Germany, celebrating a twenty-five year link. The oak tree was now ten years old. They stayed with German families and had a full programme of activities and sightseeing, including

German Scouts at Taverham Jamboree, 1961.

unveiled by Scout Christopher Green. The Scouts went on to an international jamboree, joining patrols made up of German, English, French and Dutch Scouts, and each spent a day with a host German family.

attending a football match in Dortmund to watch them play Liverpool.

In 1979, Mr Waldo Patzer, who had been presented with a Thanks Badge in 1970 for his work in international Scouting, once again came to Norwich. This time, it was on

Visiting a cave, Germany 1966. Left to right, back row: Richard Reville, Keith Norman, a Cringleford Scout, Dalmaine Dewgarde, Eddie Goldsmith. Front row: Jeremy Sayer, Paul Watts, Michael Gardner, Clive Powell, Keith Rowe, Sven (Alterna Scout hostel Leader).

Camping in Germany 1963. Left to right: Keith Goldsmith, Tony Robson, Robert Scott, Michael Butcher, Kelvin Woodard, Malcolm Braithwaite, Stewart Vaughan.

a private visit with his wife to stay with Skipper Greenfield.

Contact has again been made with Hohenlimburg as ex-Scouts and Leaders plan a nostalgic visit to Germany in their centenary year, 2008, fifty-five years since that first meeting at the Coronation Jamboree.

Archery with the German Scouts, Norwich, 1974.

Placing the plaque under the Oak Tree planted four years earlier.
Lennepark, 1969.

Close-up of the plaque which is still in place under the now mature oak tree, 2007.

Scouts travel to Germany to celebrate 25 years of friendship with the Hohenlimburg Troop, 1975.
Left to right, back row: Ventures Kevin Rowe, Stephen Green, Richard Robinson, Julian Greenfield, ASL David Beckett.
Middle row: Scouts Stephen Dunbar, ?, Gordon Chambers, John Poynter. SL Keith Rowe, GSL Alan Adcock.
Front row: Scouts Ian Mountain, Adrian Crisp, Stephen Saul, VSL Ray Crisp, Venture Richard Goodrum.

Alan Adcock at the Helm

Alan Adcock (Addy) has been Group Scout Leader since Skipper Eric Greenfield retired in 1973. Under his leadership the Group has successfully weathered the many changes that have kept Scouting relevant to the young people of the late 20th and early 21st centuries. The Scout and Cub Award Programmes have been modernised and now give more choice from a greater variety of activities, uniforms have changed for some sections, and girls are now an equal part of Scouting. In 1988 the Beaver Colony was set up for six to eight year-olds, and in 2002 Explorer Scouts for fourteen to sixteen year-olds replaced the Venture Unit.

Group Scout Leader, Alan Adcock (front left) leads the Group on Parade at the Centenary Celebrations. January 2008.

With a dedicated team of Leaders and Voluntary Helpers, the Group has always managed to run an interesting and exciting programme. All age groups have had opportunities to take part in camping and water activities, and to make a contribution to the community. They have also had considerable success in competition. Scouts have often come first or won places at regattas and, for over three decades, they have been regular winners in the District Night Hike competition.

With the help of the Parents' Committee, many fund-raising events have been organised and the money raised has contributed towards running expenses and the purchase of equipment.

There have been occasions when it was difficult to find leaders and Scout numbers have fallen, but the Group has always recovered and, for some years now, membership has been high, continuing to rise even when there was a countrywide decline.

District Commissioner, Peter Noakes presents Jonathan Gascoyne with his Queen's Scout Award. April, 1980.

All sections took part in activities to celebrate the centenary of the Scout Movement in 2007 and seven Explorer Scouts attended the World Jamboree. In 2008, the Group celebrates its own centenary with a year-long programme of events.

The 1970s

In the 1970s, as in earlier years, the Group continued to enjoy success on the water. They had several boats and canoes and took part in local and national regattas including those at Sutton Coldfield, Kingston-on-Thames, Holme Pierrepoint in Nottingham and Manchester. They went long distance canoeing and had days on the beach, swimming and water-skiing. In the summer of 1975 a party of Scouts went to Germany and hosted a return visit in 1978.

In the mid 70s Scout numbers fell but by the end of the decade there were six Patrols; so many that one had to be housed in a den outside. The Ventures also had a period of falling membership, but by 1975 there were seven Ventures and six Scouts waiting to join.

In 1977, there were more than forty Scouts who, that year, gained sixty-three proficiency badges, one hundred and one Scout Standard Awards, (including six Advanced Awards) and three Chief Scout Awards. They held nine camps, won eight medals and trophies for canoeing, took part in night hikes and went on a hike in the snow. In 1978 two boys were selected for the Norfolk Canoe Team. The next year six trophies were won at the Whitlingham regatta and first place gained at the Longridge regatta. By mid

Troop photo, 1982. Centre back: District Commissioner Stan Deeks and GSL Alan Adcock. Leaders standing. Left: Martin LeGrice and Julian Greenfield. Right: Kathryn Dulieu and Derek Page.

1979, however, the current Scout Leader, Keith Rowe, could only help part-time so the Scouts were actively looking for new leaders.

The 1980s and Girls in Scouting
In 1980, Derek Page joined as Scout Leader and the Troop again had a successful year. They went on several camps and did well in rowing and sailing competitions at local and national regattas.

Addy invests the first girl Scouts into the Troop. Left to right: Clare Boden, Hannah Smith, Katie Adcock. April 1991.

In the same year the 1st Norwich Group became an early pioneer in the move to admit girls to Scouting. Kathryn Dulieu and Sam Page were both fifteen year-olds waiting to join the Venture Unit, which was reforming after a spell with no leader. It was thought that time spent training with the Scouts before becoming Ventures would

be beneficial, so application was made to the Norfolk Scout Association for permission to enrol them as Scouts. Initially this was refused and the matter had to be referred to the National Scout Association before special permission was obtained for the girls to be invested on a trial basis.

It was not until eleven years later, in 1991, that changes were made to the Royal Charter of the Scout Association to allow girls to join the younger sections of the Movement. Soon after this the 1st Norwich Executive Committee agreed to allow girls into the Troop. Katie Adcock, Hannah Smith and Clare Boden were invested in April 1991. The first girl Cubs, Amelia Rix, Amelia Land and Hanna Burrell were invested in 2005 and, in 2006, Chloe Richardson was the first girl to join the Beaver Colony.

The early to mid 1980s were busy years, filled with camps and water activities, then, in 1988, the year of the 1st Norwich 80th Anniversary, the Group faced a crisis. For a period of over three months there was no leader or assistant to run the Scout Troop and Scout numbers fell dramatically. The Venture Unit was also without a leader and had already disbanded. Addy stood in as Leader for a time but as he was also involved with the Cubs and Beavers, he was not able to spare sufficient time to supervise the Scouts. An appeal was made through the local press for adults to help with the Group. Derek Page returned for a time to help run the Scout Troop and was later joined by Richard Cosburn who went on to become Scout Leader until mid 1991.

The 1990s
Julien Pike became Scout Leader in 1991, the year that members of the Group offered home hospitality to a party of Swedish Scouts attending the Norfolk Jamboree. By 1993 the Scouts were reported to be … *flourishing once again*. With twenty-seven Scouts, six leaders and two Venture Scouts as helpers, they were able to go on several camps and spend a lot of time canoeing in addition to other activities.

1994 was a year of high achievement. Group membership was the largest for many years. Scouts went white water canoeing, had a weekend on the MTB 102 and spent a (wet) backwoods weekend near Sheffield. They won the District Camping Competition and were placed third in the County Wayfinder Competition. In August, forty-two Group

Group Scout Leader, Alan Adcock (Addy)

Group Scout Leader since 1973, Alan has overseen the changes that have taken the Group successfully into the 21st Century and on to its Centenary in 2008. As well as implementing required organisational

Alan receives his Silver Acorn and 40 year Service Award from County Commissioner, Richard Butler, 2006.

Alan Adcock (Addy), Group Scout Leader, 1st Norwich Sea Scout Group, 2008.

changes, under his leadership the Group pioneered the admission of girls into Scouting and set up the new Beaver Colony.

He joined the 1st Norwich as a Cub in 1956 before moving up to Scouts where he became a Patrol Leader and gained his First Class Badge and Scout Cords. He helped at Cub camps and was a Cub Instructor before becoming Assistant Scout Leader in 1966.

Alan with his children Katie and Stewart Adcock at Norjam, 1995.

He received his Group Scout Leader's Wood Badge in 1988, having completed earlier Wood Badge training in the 1970s. In 1992 he was presented with the Medal of Merit and, in 1995, the Bar to Long Service for 25 years service. In 2006 he received the Silver Acorn along with his 40 year Service Award.

Alan, as a Scout at the Sandringham Jamboree, shakes hands with the Chief Scout, Sir Charles Maclean. 1964.

members went on a two-week trip to Poland. On return, they set about raising funds for twenty-four Polish Scouts to attend the 1995 Norfolk International Jamboree. In all, forty-four went to the Jamboree including Scouts, Ventures and adult Helpers.

Into the 21st century

Julian Greenfield took over as Scout Leader in 1995 and the Troop continued to take part in many activities and do well in competition despite numbers having fallen temporarily. By 1998 numbers were back up to around thirty-five Scouts and they have continued to

The winning Patrol with the Shotsilva Trophy, c1980.

remain high despite the loss of the older age group to Explorers in 2002.

Camping remains a key Scouting activity and the past twelve years have included trips to Wales, Plymouth, Longridge, Derby and, closer to home, Thetford. In 2001 Scouts took part in a Family camp with the Beavers and Cubs, and they also camped with Explorers in the New Forest. There have been walking weekends near Sheffield and Water Activities Weekends at Decoy Broad. Other activities have included abseiling, archery, air rifle shooting, canoeing and pioneering. In 2005 1st Norwich won the District football competition and in 2006 took part in the Norfolk Jamboree, as well as a particularly

cold Easter camp where they had icy tents in the morning.

District Commissioner, Malcolm Watson presents David Albury, Patrol Leader of Stags, with the Shotsilva runners-up Trophy, c1985.

District Night Hike Winners: Night Owl, Shotsilva and the County Wayfinder Competition

The District Night Hike is an annual competition, which is now called Night Owl but was formerly called Shotsilva. Teams of Scouts hike throughout the night covering a distance of about ten miles. Periodically they stop at manned bases where they have to carry out an activity, face a challenge, or deal with an incident testing their initiative, first aid and teamwork skills. The winners go on to compete in the County Wayfinders event, which is a camping competition. Here they must show a high standard of camping and are also judged on their cookery skills and the performance of tasks such as raft building, pioneering and signalling.

Photo: JULIAN NICHOLLS

Camping success for Scouts

SCOUTS in Norwich have won a top camping competition beating more than 3000 other troops in East Anglia.

The 1st Norwich Sea Scouts won through to the final of the Wayfinder camping competition having won a district and a county event.

The grand final involved 15 teams of five members from the five counties in the area.

Julian Pike, Scout leader, said: "The members of the team, three girls and two boys, had to show a high standard of camping throughout the competition.

"They were also judged on their cookery skills and had to perform tasks such as raft building, pioneering and signalling."

Members of the team are all from Lakenham based 1st Sea Scouts. They are patrol leader Aaron Bargewell, 15, assistant patrol leader Geraldine Hough, 14, Jessica Green, 14, Peter Ansell, 13 and Libby Allen, 14.

Wayfinder winners, (September 1995). Left to right: Aaron Bargewell, Peter Ansell, Geraldine Hough, Jessica Green, Libby Allen (Eastern Evening News 14-09-95).

The 1st Norwich Scouts have a long history of competing in, and often winning, the Night Hike. They have also had success in the County Wayfinder competition, especially in recent years.

Patrol Leader Milan Palmer with the Night Owl trophy, 2007.

After being awarded the runners-up trophy for Shotsilva in 1970, the Scouts went on to win first place several times in the 1970s and 80s. During the 1990s they were winners for seven consecutive years and in 1995 won the County Wayfinder competition as well. Since then they have won the Night Owl competition every year from 2003 to 2007 and the County Wayfinder competition in 2004 and 2006.

Success in this type of competition requires a high level of teamwork and leadership among the Scouts; skills they are encouraged to develop through all the various Scouting activities they undertake.

The Centenary of the Scout Movement, 2007. The Beacon of Promise

The Norfolk Scouts Beacon of Promise is an original anchor light from the SS Great Britain. It represents the spirit of Scouting throughout the world and its light spreads a greeting of friendship and peace, reminding Scouts that they are all bound by the same Promise.

During the centenary year of Scouting the lamp was passed to every Scout Group in Norfolk and, on receiving it, Scouts renewed their Promise. The 1st Norwich, as the oldest continuously running Scout Group in the county, was the first to receive it. On January 6th 2007 it was presented to Group Scout Leader Alan Adcock on the banks of the River Yare, before being rowed to the 1st Norwich Headquarters. This journey was symbolic of

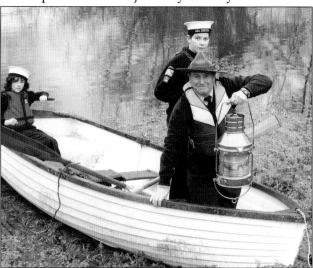

Bringing the Beacon of Promise to the 1st Norwich HQ. January, 2007. Addy wearing an original Scout hat, is rowed ashore by Milan and Alex symbolising the trip made by Baden-Powell in the 1st Norwich War Canoe in 1926.

the one made by Baden-Powell in 1926, when he travelled on the river Wensum in the 1st Norwich war canoe. At the headquarters the beacon was accepted by John Bracey, aged 83, one of the oldest known surviving 1st Norwich Scouts.

Throughout the year, the lamp made its way around the county by various modes of transport. It was returned to the 1st Norwich Group at their own Centenary Service at the Church of Saint Peter Mancroft, in January 2008, where it was handed back to the Norfolk Scout Association.

2008: The 1st Norwich Centenary Year

The 1st Norwich Sea Scout Group celebrated its Hundredth Birthday on January 15th 2008. It is one of a few Scout Groups in the country to have been running continuously since then and the oldest one in Norfolk. Celebrations commenced on 20th January with a Centenary Church Service. The Group formed a human 100 on the steps of Norwich City Hall where they released a hundred balloons in the Group colours of gold and blue, before parading to St Peter Mancroft Church.

In March a group of ex-Scouts visited Hohenlimburg in Germany, renewing a friendship with German Scouts begun in 1953. A float was entered in the Lord Mayor's

Procession in July, and there is a re-union dinner for ex-Group members in September.

Camps planned for the year include a Family Camp at Great Hautbois, Scout summer camp in Derby, and Cub camps in Norwich and Trimingham.

The Leadership

Wherever there are Scouts, Cubs or Beavers, there must be adults to organise, instruct and supervise them. Over the century there have been many leaders, helpers and parents who have given their time and skill voluntarily to the 1st Norwich Group. Their contribution is not always mentioned in the record and sometimes their names have not even been recorded, but without them the Group would not have survived. All those who have helped, in whatever capacity, remain an important part of the 1st Norwich history even though it has been possible to name only a few in this text. Following are those who lead the Group today.

Alan Adcock with daughter Katie. Katie attended her first Scout camp at 10 days old. She was one of the first girl Scouts to be invested into the Group and has been an Asst. Scout Leader since 1997, first with a troop in Wales before joining the 1st Norwich in 2001.

Jane Stafford, Asst. Group Scout Leader with granddaughter, Megan. Jane has been a Warranted Leader for 31 years. She joined the 1st Norwich in 1986 as an ACSL. Between 2000 and 2002 Jane was ADC Cubs, returning to the Group full time in 2002 as AGSL. She was awarded the Medal of Merit in 2004.

Shaun Culling, Explorer Scout Leader. Shaun is the first Leader to have progressed through all four Sections of the Group. Shaun joined as a Beaver, then went on to Cubs, Scouts and Explorers.

43

Joy Parfitt, Beaver Scout Leader. Joy has been involved since 1987, first as a Parent Helper then Secretary, becoming well known for her camp cooking skills. Joy has been a warranted Leader since 2000, when she became Beaver Scout Leader. Under her Leadership the Beavers held their first sleep-over.

Julian Greenfield, Scout Leader. Julian's dad, Eric, was the former Group Scout Leader. Julian has been involved with the Group since he joined as a Cub in 1965, taking on the role of Scout Leader in 1995. He gained the Chief Scout's 25 years Service Award in September 2003.

Neil Grogutt, Asst. Scout Leader, with son Harrison. Neil joined the 1st Norwich Scouts in 1978, having been a Cub with the Mulbarton Pack. He was Patrol Leader of the Lions before joining the Venture Unit and became a Warranted Leader in 1988. He has since gained his 20 year Chief Scout's Service Award.

Charles Bartram, Cub Scout Leader. Charles has been involved since 1960 when he became a Cub, and in all those years he hasn't missed a St George's Day parade. He has been CSL since 1978 and, before that, was ACSL for several years. Charles received the Silver Acorn Award in 2006.

Julien Pike, Asst. Scout Leader. Julien became a 1ˢᵗ Norwich Scout in 1983, taking a Leaders warrant in 1990. He was Scout Leader from 1991 to 1995.

Dean Ward, Asst. Scout Leader. Dean was a Beaver, Cub and Scout with the 11ᵗʰ Norwich, before moving to the 1ˢᵗ Norwich Scouts and then on to the Explorer Section. He took out his ASL Warrant in 2003.

Tom Porteous, Asst. Scout Leader. Tom joined in 1994 as a Scout before moving on to Ventures, becoming a Warranted Leader in 1999.

Mark Elvin, Asst. Scout Leader. Mark was a Scout and Venture Scout in Doncaster before joining the 1ˢᵗ Norwich in January, 2006.

Sara Cordy, Asst. Beaver Scout Leader with son, Cub, Oliver. Sara was a Scout herself, before becoming a Warranted Leader in 2004.

Alison Buck, Asst. Cub Scout Leader. Alison joined the Cub Pack in September 2004 as ACSL, having been a Brownie, Guide and Ranger Guide. Alison also helps out at Scout meetings when an extra female Leader is needed.

Chris Regan, Asst. Cub Scout Leader with son, Cub, Benjamin. Chris was a Parent Helper, first with the Beaver Section then the Cub Section. He became a Warranted Leader in 2004.

Alison MacNab, Asst. Beaver Scout Leader with sons, Beaver, Tristan and Cub, Jonathan. Alison has been a Warranted Leader since 2007.

Paul White, Group Treasurer, with his sons Scouts, Lewis and Alex.

Mark Robertson, Explorer Scout and Young Leader with the Cub section. Mark was a Beaver and Cub at Wymondham, but transferred to the 1st Norwich with his brothers Paul and Daniel, when his family moved to Lakenham. His father was a former 1st Norwich Scout. Mark describes Scouts as 'brilliant'.

Annette Thomas, Adult Helper with the Scout Section. For many years Annette was the Group Secretary. She gained the Chief Scouts Commendation Award in 2007.

Adrienne Hendrey, Group Chairman, with her children, Explorer Scout, Oliver and Scout, Erin.

Photographs were not available of the following Leaders: Becky Adcock, ASL; Robert Hawes, ABSL; Andy Daly and Tom Egleton, Helpers with the Cub Section.

Poland 1994

In August 1994 forty-two 1st Norwich members travelled by coach to Poland for a two-week stay with Polish Scouts. They spent a week at a camp in Golkowice before staying in the homes

The contingent for Poland, 1994. Back row: Julien Pike-Leader, David Albury, James Ambrozevich, Basil the Mascot, James Clements, Ruth Boden, Liz Ainsworth, Jane Stafford-Camp Co-ordinator, Andrew Cooke, Alison Harvey, Delia Hough, Julian Greenfield, Douglas Hough, Stewart Adcock, Steve Christopher, Danny Willcox, Colin Hough.
Middle row: Sally Denham, Liz Perry, Richard Gover, Sarah Ainsworth, Ellen Green, Katie Adcock, Michael Denham, Graham Hough, Daniel Perry, Tom Porteous, Geraldine Hough, Paul Guttridge, Jamie Clarke.
Front row: Jessica Green, Aaron Bargewell, Alex Swinbourne, Jon Armes, Tom Christopher, William Perry, Laura Bargewell, Laura Godfrey, Mark Ambrozevich.
Missing from photograph: Dave Swinbourne and Clare Boden.

of Polish Scouts at Nova Huta near Krakow. The party was made up of Scouts, Ventures, Leaders, Parent Helpers and two coach drivers. The trip, led by Scout Leader Julien Pike (Camp Leader) and Assistant Cub Scout Leader Jane Stafford (Camp Co-ordinator), was the culmination of eighteen months of planning and fund-raising by the Group.

The journey took two days, with an overnight stop at a Youth Hostel in Eisenbach, in eastern Germany. It was uneventful until, after crossing the Polish border, progress was considerably slowed by the uneven surface of the E4 motorway - the coach driver even felt it necessary to remove the hub caps to prevent them being dislodged and lost. When the motorway suddenly ended in a pile of earth, cross-country navigation was needed to find the way to Krakow and the camp-site at Golkowice. On arrival at midnight, seven hours later than expected, the coach was unable to get through the low gateway erected by the Polish Scouts and had to be left outside for the night.

There were two hundred Scouts camping at the site in a wooded area with log cabins set among the trees. Facilities were basic with a river for swimming but no hot water for showers. Meals were served in a canteen and proved to be interesting and different. The English Scouts had to get used to eating bread, salad and sausage for both breakfast and evening meal, with a hot meal at lunch-time. On one occasion, the English contingent cooked shepherd's pie and apple crumble for the Polish Scouts. It went down well except for the bitter lime jelly they had bought to go with the crumble thinking it was custard powder.

Relaxing outside one of the log cabins.

Raft trip on the Dunajec river.

The week was spent in Scouting activities and sight-seeing. There was a football match, a nine-mile hike to climb the highest mountain in Poland - the Three Crowns Mountain, and a raft trip down the Dunajec river. There were camp-fires and singing in the evenings and the groups exchanged songs and chants. A music festival was organised at which Norwich won the prize for the best international performance. Their loudness and enthusiasm made up for any lack of musical talent although it must be added that they were the only international competitor.

Impromptu conga in Zakopane.

An overnight trip was made to Zakopane in the Tartra Mountains. Scouts took a cable car to the top of a mountain and some of them hiked on the way down. At the top they were able to stand with one foot in Poland and one in Slovakia. There were two casualties on this trip who received hospital attention, one for a cut leg and one for heat-stroke.

Heat-stroke and dehydration were problems throughout the stay in Poland with several members of the party affected. Temperatures were high, sometimes over 40 degrees centigrade. The camp water was unpalatable so large quantities of bottled water were provided to try to encourage the Scouts to drink enough fluid.

While in Zakopane, a visit was made to the grave of the founder of Polish Scouting where 1st Norwich joined the Polish Scouts in a short service and members of the Group re-affirmed their Scout Promise.

Scouts stand with one foot in Poland and one in Slovakia.

The grave of the Founder of Polish Scouting

Back at Golkowice, they met the Scouts from Nova Huta with whom they were going to stay. They had a lot of fun joining in a traditional Polish camp activity of 'The Weddings' where Scouts dress up, choose partners and marry each other for the duration of the camp.

William, James, Aaron and Richard prepare for the 'wedding ceremonies'.

Katie, Jon and Julien hand gifts to the Polish Commandant.

Three days were spent in Nova Huta staying at the homes of Polish Scouts. There was sight-seeing around Kracow and visits to a salt mine and Auschwitz. The Leaders met with the local Polish Commandant, discussing the way forward for Scouting in Poland and extending an invitation to the Polish Scouts to visit Norwich in 1995. A final camp-fire, where Auld Lang Syne was sung in both Polish and English, ended a happy and successful visit. On the ferry back across the English Channel, ten Scouts successfully completed a challenge to obtain a tour of the bridge and have their photo taken with the Captain.

The Group subsequently raised funds to enable twenty-four Polish Scouts to come to Norwich to enjoy home hospitality and attend the

Jamie, Sarah, Clare, Douglas, James, Julien, Jane, Katie and Paul meet the Captain.

International Jamboree at the Norfolk Show Ground in 1995. (Reports by Julien Pike and Jane Stafford.)

Polish and 1st Norwich Sea Scouts at the Norfolk Jamboree, the Royal Norfolk Showground, 1995.

The Colours

The Group Flag, or the Colours as it is known, symbolizes the brotherhood of Scouts, serving as a reminder of the ideals and commitments made through the Scout Promise and the Scout Law. The flag is usually dedicated, or blessed, in church on presentation to the Troop and thereafter must be treated with respect and reverence, being escorted by a Colour Party when moved. The Colours are regularly carried at Church Parades, and used at the investiture of new members and other significant occasions.

The original 1st Norwich Colours were made by Mrs Edward Coe and presented to the Troop in 1924. A dedication service was later led by the Vicar at St Thomas' Church in Earlham Road.

The Colours were made of heavy silk, embroidered with a design drawn by one of the Scout Leaders. They had taken two years to complete and Skipper Coe wrote of the love and patience with which his mother undertook the work, including a trip to London to find the right material. He tells of the pride they took in the Colours and of what they meant to the Troop. They were their … *proudest possession … a sacred and invaluable trust* which they embraced with … *pride engendered by reverence.*

The new Flag (Troop Colours) c1924.

Mrs Coe later backed the Colours with a replica of the design on the front. She re-presented them to the Troop at a ceremony held at Headquarters on Remembrance Day 1930. In response the Troop gave her the affectionate

Mrs Coe re-presenting the newly backed Colours, 1930.

Flag with poles carved by T W Killick, 1933.

title of 'Auntie' and from then on always addressed her as such.

Rover Scout Tom W Killick carved a pole for the Colours in oak. On it he carved the history of the Troop together with the names of Troop members who had been killed in the First World War.

In 1952, on the Silver Jubilee of their original dedication, the Colours, by now embellished with the badges of all the international jamborees at which the Troop was represented, were re-dedicated at Christ Church, Eaton by the Reverend Hurd.

"IT CAN BE DONE"

After sixty-eight years of service, the Colours were replaced by a new Group Flag which was made by Skipper Coe's widow, Maidie Coe and their daughter Georgina Thomas. It was dedicated with a service at Old Lakenham Church on 28th June, 1992.

When the Cubs and Beavers take part in parades they now also carry their own Flags; the Cub Pack having had theirs since 1957.

At the Dedication Service, 28th June, 1992.

Maidie Coe shows the new Colours, 1992.

The original flag on which were sewn the early Jamboree badges.

The Group at the Dedication Service, Old Lakenham Parish Church, June 1992.

St George's Day

Baden-Powell designated St George as the Patron Saint of Scouting after referring to the legend of the Knights of the Round Table in 'Scouting for Boys'. He felt that Scouts should show the same determination in the face of difficulty and strive to

Hay Hill, 1933.

Colour Party on City Hall steps, 1953. Left to right: Cub ?, Senior Scout John Webster, Scout Lenny Aldridge.

Outside Norwich Cathedral, 1937.

It has become a tradition to have a photograph of the Group taken on St George's Day, often on the steps of City Hall.

overcome fear to act bravely, as St George had done when he slew the dragon. He said that

> *… no matter how great or how terrifying (a difficulty) may appear. (A Scout) should go at it boldly and confidently … to try and overcome it …and the probability is that he will succeed.*

Every year, on the nearest Sunday to St George's Day (April 23rd), ceremonies are held throughout the United Kingdom where Scouts reaffirm their Promise and acknowledge the Scout Law.

For many years the 1st Norwich Group has joined with others in the District for a Parade starting at City Hall. A different Group each year provides the main Colour Party. After an address by the Lord Mayor, each Norwich District marches to its allotted church for a service during which they renew their Scout Promise.

The Group, 1958. Standing, left to right: Scout Flag Bearer, Julian O'Dell; Leaders, Fred Jones, Eric Greenfield, Basil Craske, Dinah Higham; Cub Flag Bearer, Malcolm Braithwaite.

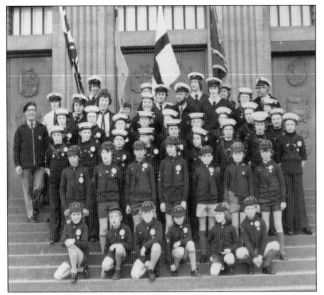

*The Group on City Hall steps, 1977. Leaders present include:
Charles Bartram, Maureen Staff, Alan Adcock, Eddie
Goldsmith, Keith Rowe, Dave Reyner.*

*Colour Party on City Hall steps 1977. Left to right: Venture
Richard Goodrum, Scout Leslie Hill, Cub Jonathan Copping,
Scout Ian Mountain.*

*Cubs on St. George's Day, 1979. Includes A Keeley,
S Skitmore, S Hindle, D Moore, S Forster, A Wienle, D Howard,
J Jarvis, A Waller, I Moore.*

*Colour Party St Georges Day, 2000.
Scout Shaun Culling, Cub Nathan Quarmby,
Beaver ?.*

*The Group at Norwich Cathedral, 1990. Leaders, left to right, back row: Julien Pike,
Richard Cosburn, Glynnis Clements, David Albury, Danny Willcox, Alan Adcock,
Charles Bartram, Jane Stafford. Front left: Jenny Smith.*

1st Norwich Cubs perform a 'sketch' at the St George's Day Service in Norwich Cathedral, c2000.

The Group on the City Hall steps, April 2007. Scout Flag Bearer, Greg Beaumont; Cub Flag Bearer, Megan Rickards; Beaver Flag Bearer, Max Reeves. Leaders present are: Dean Ward, Mark Elvin, Neil Grogutt, Tom Porteous. Shaun Culling, Katie Adcock, Julian Greenfield, Jane Stafford, Alan Adcock, Charles Bartram, Joy Parfitt, Chris Regan, Alison Buck, Alison MacNab, Sara Cordy.

Guards of Honour

Throughout their history, Scouts have formed Guards of Honour on ceremonial occasions and the happiest of these have been at weddings of Scout Leaders. Less happily, in the early years, when life expectancy was shorter, they were sometimes called upon to attend funerals of fellow Scouts. The Troop registers record several young Scouts as having died by showing the tracking sign for "gone home".

Right: The wedding of Bernard High (Bunny) and Miss Gladys Parker, at the Baptist Church, Unthank Road. April 1934.

Edward Coe's wedding to Miss Winifred Lemmon (Maidie). The Church of St Peter Mancroft, June 1935.

Scout Leader Frank Folkard (Nunky) married Miss Peggy Bateson, at St Augustine's Church, June 1952.

Cubs at the wedding of Cub Leader Charles Bartram and Emma Farrow with Assistant Cub Leader, Sheila Hughes on the right. April 1976.

Scout Leader Keith Rowe and Moira Youngman, married at Fritton Church, Long Stratton, October 1978.

Above: At the wedding of Venture Scout Leader Derek Page and Kathryn Dulieu, September 1986. Scouts left to right: Stewart Adcock, Richard Smith, David Albury, Danny Willcox, Philip Woods.

Right: Cubs at the wedding of Assistant Cub Leader Jane Blyth and Reg Stafford, June 1996. With them, Cub Leader Charles Bartram, left and Assistant Cub Leader David Albury, right.

The funeral of Scout Bales, 1915.

The funeral cortège at the cemetery. Scouts pulling the funeral bier.

Anniversaries

In 1929, a parchment was sent to the Chief Scout to commemorate the 21st Anniversary of the founding of the 1st Norwich Scout Group. Drafted by a member of the Junior Troop, it depicted various emblems and was signed by all members of the Group. A reply signed by Robert Baden-Powell, was promptly received, in which he highly congratulated the young artist on having produced such a splendid piece of work.

Golden Jubilee

In 1958, a dinner was held at the Flixton Rooms, Norwich, to mark the 50th Anniversary of the Group. The Eastern Evening News reported on the 28th January, that *It was a night for reminiscing* ... for ... *many people who had not met for nearly half a century.*

The Group President, Mr Edward Coe, was presented with a wooden ash-tray by Mr W. T. Barber, the longest serving active 1st Norwich Scout. It was engraved with the Group's emblem and inscribed 'To Skipper, from his old Scouts of the 1st Norwich'.

The Deputy Lord Mayor of Norwich, Mr Eric Hinde, himself a former 1st Norwich Scout, presented an emblem carved by another former Scout, Mr Harold Clarke, to the Scout Master Mr E A Greenfield.

Above: Parchment sent to Sir Robert Baden-Powell on the 21st anniversary of the Troop, 1929.
Right: Reply received from Sir Robert Baden-Powell, 1929.

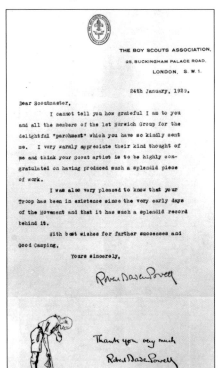

Fifteen German Scouts from Hohenlimburg attended the dinner. A commemorative booklet was produced, which included the Group Song written by E Coe, a Diary of Events, and a List of Patrol Leaders and Troop Leaders from 1908 to 1957. A birthday tea was held the next day with a cake with fifty candles.

The Group has continued to mark significant anniversaries with a Thanksgiving Service and re-unions for ex-members. In 2008, the Centenary Year, the celebrations commenced with a Service at St Peter Mancroft Church, followed by a year of further events.

Golden Jubilee dinner at the Flixton Rooms, Norwich, 1958. Front table, facing camera 2nd & 3rd left, Mark & Georgina Coe, 6th left, Eric Greenfield.

Alan Adcock leads the Parade to Old Lakenham Parish Church for the 66th Birthday Thanksgiving Service. January 1974.

Display in the window of the Leeds and Holbeck Building Society. Organised by Charles Bartram on the 75th Anniversary, 1983.

The Group on the 80th Anniversary, 1988. Present are Maidie Coe and the Lord Mayor of Norwich.

Float in the Lord Mayor's Procession on the 85th Anniversary. July, 1993. Seated in canoe, left to right: James Ambrozevich and James Clements.

Ex-Scout Derek Young cutting the cake at the 90th anniversary, 1998. Others left to right: David Albury, Charles Bartram, Julian Greenfield, Harold Herrman, an ex-Scout from Germany, ex-Scout Allan Abel, Julien Pike, Alan Adcock, Jane Stafford.

GSL Alan Adcock invests Jack and Rose Pearson at the 90th Anniversary Thanksgiving Service. January, 1998.

Above: Beavers, Cubs and Scouts celebrate the 95th Anniversary. January 2003. Left to right, Scouts: Christopher Lodge, Elizabeth Lloyd-Wickens, Charlton Palmer, Sophia Wincup, William Walker, William Saunders. Cubs: Jack Gilbert, Alex Lloyd-Wickens, Oliver Rox, Oliver Hendry, Alex Saunders. Beavers: Billy Farrow, Owen Cunningham.

Left: Beavers, Cubs, Scouts and Explorers form a 'human 100' on the steps of City Hall at their centenary. January, 2008.

The Headquarters Story: From Cliff House to Old Lakenham

The 1st Norwich Scouts have long enjoyed excellent facilities for Scouting thanks to their own keenness and the enthusiastic support of other people associated with the Group. From 1914 onwards they have had their own headquarters in Norwich and, for two periods in their history, additional Sea Scout headquarters at Wroxham Broad (1926-1936 and 1948-1955).

When they first started, Lion Patrol had the run of a copse at Cliff House, even being tolerated when … *in their exuberance they cut down a valuable tree.* (Edward Coe, Memoirs). Later, Kangaroo Patrol met in a shed they called the 'Club House' in the grounds of 'Homestead', the Coe family home in Unthank Road.

When established as St Thomas' (1st Norwich) Troop in 1912, they met at St Thomas' Parish Hall in Earlham Road, but by 1913 the success of the Troop and growing numbers saw them looking to find a permanent headquarters of their own with more room for Scouting activities.

The 'Log Cabin,' Recreation Road
In 1914 Mr J G Bower gave the Troop use of a small plot of land in a field adjoining Recreation Road. Here they placed a building and extension measuring in total fifty feet by twelve. Named the Log Cabin, it was officially opened on December 19th by the Rev W F Brown,

The Troop outside the "Log Cabin" 1917.

60

Headmaster of Norwich School and President of the Troop.

Before the end of the First World War members of the Troop were making plans to extend their accommodation and by 1920 they had a separate den for the leaders, a library, a canteen and a den for the newly formed Rover Patrol. The Scouts themselves worked on maintaining the buildings, reporting in October 1920 that they had been repairing windows and painting the library ceiling. The accounts for 1921 show the building was valued at £100. With 40 members and no room to take new recruits, the Troop set about raising money for additional accommodation. A Headquarters fund was started and by 1923 this stood at £73.

The Move to Jessopp Road
In 1923 the Troop moved to Jessopp Road. They leased half an acre of land between Glebe Road and Colman Road from the Ecclesiastical Commissioners. The old Headquarters was moved and re-erected with additional premises at a cost of over £100. It was opened in December 1923, by the Scoutmaster's parents, Mr and Mrs Edward Coe senior. They had generously made good a deficit of £60, which had been paid for an army hut that in Skipper Coe's words 'went west'.

The new main building was 115 feet long, divided into 14 rooms. Alfred Buttle (Sandy) described it as an ex-Army hut with extensions set in rough ground next to the allotments. As the Group expanded they knocked down a piggery to make more room. There was a club-room, a main hall, part of which was used as a gym, a Court of Honour with log seats, patrol dens and a workshop for the Seniors. An extension was built with dens for the Cubs. Each one had its own small entrance set at ground level so that Shere Khan the tiger (and most adults) could not enter. Inside, was … *beautiful woodwork* to which Cubs fixed their own decorations.

Scouts continued to take responsibility for some of the maintenance of the buildings. In 1924 Stag Patrol reported that they had finished boarding and decorating their patrol den. The dens were used on wet days and for the Patrol in Council with wardens appointed to see that they were kept tidy.

In the grounds were patrol camp sites, a shelter for canoes, a tripod for climbing and a Kraal for Wood Badge training. A camp-fire dell was dug in 1925. T W Killick (Chuck) remembered digging it and planting plum bushes round the

Ready for a Church Parade. Jessopp Road HQ c1925.

Road was at the time, especially in the winter months, 'Bunny' High described the site as ...*a pinnacle of youthful enterprise and solid Scouting amongst a myriad of allotments.*

When the lease expired in 1930 the Troop was able to renew it annually until, in 1933, it was finally terminated and the land released for development.

Old Lakenham Hall
The Norfolk Scout Association converted Old Lakenham Hall and its grounds into their

top of the site where the patrols had gardens. He and other ex-Scouts remembered eating crisps and chocolate from the canteen, which was housed in a ... *handsome oak cabinet.*

As well as attending meetings and weekend camps, Scouts spent much of their leisure time at the Headquarters. Patrol Leaders had access to the keys to open the building when required.

Patrol gardens at Jessopp Road HQ, 1925.

They played games such as shin hockey and pursued other activities, some of which may not have been sanctioned by those in authority. One Scout was said to have airguns and a bored-out starting pistol, and some were known to have ridden a motorbike down Jessopp Road. (This may have been Skipper Coe's much-loved motor bike, Scotty.) The Fire Brigade were called on one occasion when the Rover den caught fire. A wall was burnt through and the piano damaged by water. The cost of repairs was £20-25.

Remembering how dark and lonely Jessopp

A Wolf Cub on the Climbing Tripod, 1925.

Headquarters and Training Centre in 1932. They leased the Hall for a nominal rent from Dr Oliver Gurney of Oxford until, in 1959, they were given the first option to purchase. £3,750 was raised through a local appeal and Government

Edward Coe, 1st Norwich Group President (standing), at the handover of the title deeds of Old Lakenham Hall to the Norfolk Boy Scouts' Association, September 1960.

61

Cubs on Skipper Coe's motor bike, 1926.

grants, and the title deeds were handed over at a ceremony held on 25th September 1960. (Eastern Evening News, September 26th,1960)

In 1932, Edward Coe, who was District Commissioner at the time, moved to a flat in the Hall. It was to be his home, and that of his family after his marriage in 1935, for around fifteen years. During 1934 the 1st Norwich Group moved, somewhat reluctantly, to the Hall from their old headquarters in Jessopp Road. On arrival, they made a resolve to settle in and become part of their new neighbourhood.

Maidie Lemmon lays the second brick, 1935.

The Scouts met in the Hall until a new Headquarters was built for them near the stables and outhouses. Ex-Scouts remember spending the winter cleaning up second-hand bricks to be used in the building and in January 1935 Mrs Edward Coe (Auntie) laid the foundation stone. Skipper Coe's fiancée, Miss Maidie Lemmon, also laid a brick. The new building provided a den for each patrol as well as facilities for activity and craft work.

Scouts enjoyed a lot of freedom in the large grounds and on the river. There were permanent field kitchens, an old mock windmill near the

Old Lakenham Hall from the river. To the left the windmill and to the right the climbing frame. Centre, can be seen the meadow used for camping.

water, and a climbing frame. At one time a miniature rifle range was constructed at the back of the Hall, and for a while a pony called Kim was kept in the stables near the windmill.

Two large carved totems, Mr Can and Mr Can't, stood guard at the entrance to the camp-fire circle. These were later placed outside the Hall and eventually moved to the current Norfolk Scout Association Headquarters at Eaton Vale.

Each patrol had its own Canadian canoe, which they had to maintain. Scouts played wide games over wild areas in Coopers

Mr Can, one of two large carved totem poles forming the camp fire gateway.

Lane, Sandy Lane and the marshes. Axes and sheath knives were standard equipment at the time. David Baxter tells the story of a Scout sitting on the wrong side of a branch while cutting it from a tree over the river. He fell into three feet of mud and had to be rescued.

Digging trenches for the water supply to HQ, 1950s.

By the 1950s the building was in constant need of maintenance so a repair/replacement fund was started and improvements were made. The fireplace was removed from the Cub den and a gas heater installed. A new water supply was laid on and a kitchen installed. Much of the work, including digging trenches for the pipes, was undertaken by Senior Scouts, Leaders and parents.

The Group now sought to formalise their tenancy with the Norfolk Scout Association. An agreement was reached whereby they would pay rent of £5 per annum while retaining responsibility for the upkeep of the building and the dividing wall. They were still able to use the grounds of the Hall for Scouting activities, only needing to give notice when they wished to do so. However, they were reminded that in view of the fact they were based in the grounds of County Headquarters, they were expected to maintain the highest standards of tidiness and appearance.

Towards the end of the decade parents of the Scouts re-surfaced the roof of the headquarters building. The father and brother of Scout

Foundations for the present HQ. 1967.

Peter Martin (Cox'un), who had been killed in an accident in 1948, gave their labour in his memory. Such was his love of Scouting he is buried in Lakenham Churchyard overlooking the headquarters with the Rover Scout badge engraved on his headstone.

Ex-Scouts also worked on the quay heading at this time, having to negotiate with the River Commissioners, who felt they had taken more ground than they were entitled to.

A new building

By 1965 the Group were ready to build a new Headquarters. They had £2400 in the kitty and planning permission to go ahead. Disappointingly, they were unable to start work until the following year due to a credit squeeze imposed by the Government of the time. Building eventually commenced in late 1966 and while work was going on the Scouts held their meetings in the Old Hall.

Grave of Peter Martin, showing the Rover Scout emblem.

Official opening of new HQ by Mrs Maidie Coe, May 1967.

Climbing frame erected in the 1960s.

Scouts preparing to go on the water, c1980. The boat 'Lady G' in the background.

Parents and ex-Scouts gave help with painting, decorating and panelling the main hall and work was completed by May 1967. The new Headquarters was officially opened by Mrs Maidie Coe in August 1967.

Furniture, presented by the Guild of Old Scouts as a memorial to Skipper Coe, who had died in 1964, was installed in the Court of Honour.

The sale of Old Lakenham Hall

In 1977, after more than forty years as the Norfolk Scout Association County Headquarters, Old Lakenham Hall was sold for development.

The 1st Norwich Group were able to retain their Headquarters in part of the grounds of the Hall although the change caused them some difficulties. They no longer had access to the old toilet block and the Senior Scout (Venture) den above it. They lost their current entrance and also the use of the extensive grounds of the Old Hall.

Negotiation with the developers by Group Scout Leader Alan Adcock resulted in an entrance with space enough to move boats in and out. New toilets were added and later a new boat shed was built.

The building is still in use today although plans are under way to raise funds to upgrade or replace it in the not too distant future. A new climbing tower was built in the grounds in 2002 to replace the one which had been erected in 1969.

Canoeing at HQ, 1981.

The new climbing/abseiling tower, 2005.

The Cub Story

From the beginning of the Scout Movement, boys all over the country who were too young to be enrolled as Scouts simply turned up at meetings and joined in Troop activities. With the aim of formalising and controlling this unofficial participation, the 1st Norwich Troop, in 1911, agreed that younger boys could take part in some of their activities.

In 1916, Baden-Powell published the Wolf Cub scheme to cater for eight to eleven year olds. Packs of Wolf Cubs were split into Sixes, each led by a Sixer and a Second, sometimes with a Senior Sixer. The Pack Leader was called Akela and the programme of activities was based around stories from The Jungle Book by Rudyard Kipling.

Wolf Cubs wore a yellow scarf and yellow-piped, green cap. They had their own salute and handshake, their own law and promise, and they aimed at gaining their First and Second Stars and various proficiency badges. Work towards the badges was based on activities that contributed to physical development, personal care and knowledge of the natural world, as well as fire lighting, tying knots and craftwork. When Cubs had earned their Stars, they wore them on their caps to signify that they had both eyes open.

The 1st Norwich Wolf Cub Pack was started in May 1920, and in August the boys' mothers were invited to attend the first investitures led by Edward Coe. Some of the Cubs were recruited from the Preparatory Section of the City of Norwich School. Among them was T W Killick (Chuck), who went on to maintain a life-long interest in Scouting.

Senior Sixer, Peter White wearing Cub uniform, 1957. The two stars on his cap signify he has his eyes wide open.

Miss Mary Easton took on the role of Cub Mistress in 1921 with two Sixes named the Red and Grey Wolves. Her assistant, William Middleton, took over from her to become Cub Master in 1923. Pack meetings were held at Scout headquarters and, after the move to Jessopp Road in 1923, the Sixes were given their own dens. Alfred Buttle (Sandy) remembers sitting around a big tortoise stove at the end of Pack nights with the leaders reading or telling stories. He became a Cub in 1928 after his older brother, Ted, had taken him to meet the Rover Crew. They taught him how to use a bow and arrow and, after hitting a bulls-eye and being impressed by their Sea Scout sweaters, he determined to become a Rover Scout one day. He achieved this ambition and went on to become Scoutmaster for a period in the late 1940s.

Miss Mary Easton, 1922.

In 1921 the Cubs went on their first camp with the Scouts and took part in the Annual Troop Concert. In 1922 they came third in the Ambulance Shield and participated in the Cub Games before Prince Henry at the Norwich Scout Association Rally at Crown Point. In the same year they also entered the District Totem Pole Competition, which they went on to win in 1924, 1926 and 1928.

They were presented with the Totem Pole by the Chief Scout, Sir Robert Baden-Powell, at the County Rally at Mousehold Aerodrome in June 1926. The pole, with a wolf's head at the top, was used at Pack meetings and in ceremonies. It carried a record of the Pack's achievements in the form of attached ribbons, on which were the names of all the Cubs and the badges they had earned. The Cubs still have a Totem Pole, which today is used in the opening and closing ceremonies at Pack meetings.

Membership of the Cub Pack grew so that in 1927 it was felt necessary to limit the number to eighteen. Records for this period are incomplete but indicate that Neville Coe (Bosun) was Cub Master for some years around this time and he also played a role at District level. He was still Cub Master in 1932.

Bernard High (Bunny) was Cub Master in 1936 when, on the occasion of the annual bonfire and firework display at Old Lakenham Hall, he noticed a Cub floating in the river. On going to his rescue while wearing a jacket and rubber boots, he himself got stuck in the mud. Luckily someone else managed to get the boy out of the water and Bunny was able to swim to the diving stage and climb out.

In 1957, at the instigation of Cub Master Fred Jones (Bosun), the Cubs received their own Colours, presented to them at a short ceremony conducted by Mr Mollet, who was Chairman of the Group Committee at the time.

Throughout the late 1950s and early 1960s Pack membership rose until there were forty-three

A Cub in uniform c1944 (Bernard Mason).

Cubs. During this time, with Dinah Higham as Cub Leader and Mary Palmer Assistant Cub Leader, the Pack undertook a number of ambitious activities, including outings, camps and a series of concerts. In 1958, a successful concert was given at a Senior Citizens Club in Sprowston. In 1959 they put on a Nativity Play and in 1961, they performed for the public as well as at a Senior Citizens Club and a home for boys. In December 1962, a public concert was staged for three nights at Duke Street Central Youth Hall. The takings from this were used to fund a Christmas party and to contribute to the new headquarters building fund. Cub concerts still feature as a Pack activity, especially at Christmas.

In 1961 the Cubs went on four camps, one held at Ringland, from which they made daily visits to the international Scout camp at Taverham, and another, attended by twenty-four Cubs, at Buckmore Park in Kent. In 1962 the Pack holiday was held at Budleigh Salterton in Devon where one young Cub on his first trip away from home suffered badly from homesickness. His name was Charles Bartram and he is now the Pack Akela. That same year Cubs were awarded twelve 1st Stars, thirteen 2nd Stars, one hundred and eighty proficiency badges and thirteen Leaping Wolf badges, which was a link badge between Cubs and Scouts.

The Cub programme was revised nationally in 1966. With the aim of building stronger ties between Packs and

Sir Robert Baden-Powell presents the Totem Pole, 1926.

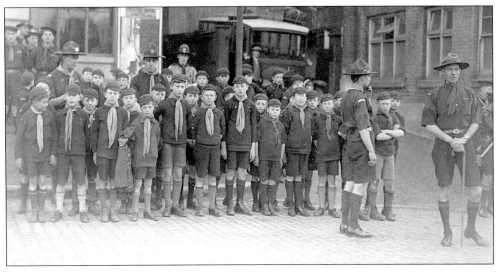

1st and 2nd Norwich Cub Packs, 1929.

Cubs with the Troop at Jessopp Road HQ, 1933.

Scout Troops, Wolf Cubs became Cub Scouts and a wider range of activities was introduced. Cubs now worked towards Bronze, Silver and Gold Arrows instead of two Stars. This was modified ten years later as the Developed Arrow Scheme,

Charles Bartram took over from Mrs Fischer in 1978 after serving for a period as an Assistant Leader. He has continued to lead the Cub Pack ever since, delivering an action-packed programme with help from many enthusiastic and able assistants, in particular Jane Stafford (formerly Blyth) and David Albury, who were both Assistant Cub Leaders for several years.

1983 was a typically busy year for the Cubs when, among other activities, they camped at Eaton Vale and three of them went on a Challenge Day with Scouts and Ventures. They also spent a memorable day boating at Decoy Broad, during the course of which Cubs watched in amazement as their Leader, Charles, managed to capsize the 470 sailing boat while it was still tied up at the dock.

The Cub programme changed again when the Challenge and Adventure scheme replaced the Developed Arrow scheme in 1991. It was to provide a more structured programme with more compulsory activities.

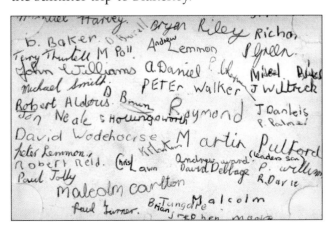
Cub Pack, 1959.

which gave Cubs a greater choice within the range of activities.

Cub numbers fell dramatically during the mid-1960s before rising again. Mrs Fischer became Cub Scout Leader in 1968 and by 1974 there were thirty-six Cubs when a full coach load went on the summer trip to Blakeney.

Cub signatures on a postcard sent to Assistant Cub Leader Alan Adcock, whilst he was in hospital. c1960.

Akela, Mrs Fischer, left, presents Ian and Paul with leaving cakes in 1978 when they emigrated to New Zealand. Mrs Staff and Addy look on.

Cub Pack with Leaders Sheila Hughes and Charles Bartram, 1983.

The Membership Badge, Cub Scout Award, Adventure Award and Adventure Crest Award were introduced to act as a continuous link between Beavers, Cubs and Scouts. In addition, the Cub Scout Challenge Badge for Cubs in their final year was to provide adventurous activities like those undertaken by Scouts and to emphasise the role of leadership. Proficiency badges were renamed Activity badges and

Charles at Halloween, c1978.

Jane Stafford presented Christopher Bolton, Lance Annison, Christopher Lower, Marc Beall, Andrew Fletcher, Daniel Royal, Robert Smith with their Challenge Award, May 1994.

more were introduced. The scheme was modified in 1995 and the Road Safety Badge introduced.

During the 1990s the Cubs went on many camps and outings as well as taking part in other activities such as abseiling, canoeing, hiking and working towards badges. In 1994 seven Cubs received their Challenge Badge after completing a series of challenges such as hiking, orienteering and map reading. A year later all the Cubs had completed their Personal Safety badge.

On the occasion of the Cub Scouts' national 80th birthday in 1996, the Pack took part in a nationwide challenge to travel 'Around the world in 80 days'. This involved the Cubs completing a number of challenges over a three-month period: they climbed the equivalent height of the Eiger, completing 4,100 metres in a series of runs of 250 metres each, up the steps from King Street to Bracondale at Carrow Hill in Norwich. At a Gladiator Games night they negotiated an obstacle course made from such things as chairs, sheeting, poles and skittles. They competed in a camel race where each Cub made a wooden camel on wheels and, wearing a traditional fez, raced over sand piles and rocks. At a Festival of Light they made boats which they set sail on the river, each carrying a lighted candle. They collected a mile of copper coins in a local store, raising £768.00 for Children in Need and Group funds. Five of the Cubs presented the cheque at Radio Norfolk.

Charles Bartram celebrated twenty-five years of service as Cub Leader in 1999. During

Jane presents Charles with a commemorative cake, to mark his 25th year as 'Akela', 1999.

the same year Cubs were awarded twenty proficiency badges, seven Cub Scout Awards, and five Adventure Crest Awards. They also made a trip to Legoland and went on a night walk around Norwich.

Since the turn of the century the Cub programme has been as full and varied as ever. Time has been spent learning new skills and working towards a variety of badges including those for explorer, home help, handyman, naturalist, scientist, cook, artist and astronomer. Among other activities, the Cubs have tried carpentry, craft-work, bird watching, rifle shooting and canoeing. They have had days out and taken part in Pack and District night-hikes and sleepovers. In the year 2000 seventy-six Cubs took part in a District night hike based at the 1st Norwich headquarters. There have been bonfires and parties at Christmas, as well as Christmas plays, often held in conjunction with the Beavers. Eighty children attended a disco held in the year 2000.

In 2004, Assistant Cub Leader, David Albury left to take part in the 2004-2005 Global Challenge Round the World Yacht Race. Using the internet, Cubs were able to follow

and chart the progress of his ten-month journey on the winning boat, BG Spirit.

Camping has given Cubs the opportunity to put into practice skills such as fire lighting, cooking on open fires, and knotting. They have camped at Thetford and Trimingham and also attended District camps. They went to the Cub Jamboree at the Norfolk Showground in 2001, took part in the District Totem Pole event in 2003, attended the County Cub

Charles Bartram as a Cub, 1961.

camp in 2005, and came second in a County Cooking competition in 2006.

The first girls joined the Pack in September 2005. They were Amelia Rix, Amelia Land and Hanna Burrell.

Winners of the District Cooking Competition, who went on to be one of two teams to represent the County of Norfolk in the Regional Final, 2006. Standing left to right: Daniel Gentle, Megan Rickards, Amelia Land, Ross Gilbert, Daniel Venn. Kneeling front: Katie Knights, Oliver Truswell.

"IT CAN BE DONE"

With the rest of the Group, Cubs took part in the Beacon of Promise ceremony to celebrate the centenary of the Scout Movement in 2007, and in January 2008 joined in the celebrations for the Group's own 100th birthday.

Right: Taking part in the Beacon of Promise ceremony. January 2007. Left to right: Former 1st Norwich Scout, John Bracey; Cub, Daniel Venn; Beaver, Domynyk Belcher; Deputy County Commissioner (Youth Programme), Alan Thorp; Scout, Josee Tisdale; other Cubs.

Rovers, Ventures and Explorers

Rovers

Rover Scouts were first established nationally in 1918 in order to provide continuing interest and recognition for Senior Scouts, especially those who had served in the First World War. A Rover Patrol was made up of Scouts over 17 years of age and led by an elected Rover Mate. Their motto was Brotherhood and the Community and their objective was to give Service - to Self, the Scout Movement and the Community.

The 1st Norwich Troop established their first Rover Patrol in 1919 with C G Coleman as Rover Mate. They met three times a month and by early

Rovers helping at camp, c1923.

1920 had built themselves a Rover Den at Scout Headquarters.

The Rovers, and later the Sea Rovers, worked jointly with the Scouts but also organised additional outings and camps of their own. In the spirit of Service, they assisted with the work of the 1st Norwich and other Scout Troops. In their first year they helped at the Scouts' summer camp near Lowestoft, walking miles each day to buy fresh provisions.

In 1928 four Rovers under the supervision of Arthur Nicholls (Honorary Scout Master of the Troop from 1914 to 1919), spent a useful and instructive week gaining valuable sailing experience aboard the yacht Ripple III. In the same year a party of eight Rovers went to the second National Rover Moot near Birmingham. They travelled in two cars, carrying their luggage in the dicky seat of one. On the way they camped for the night in a lane near Swaffham and arrived

Rover camp at Stoke Holy Cross. Glaxo, Flop Thurless and Neville Coe, c1925.

Rover Service Patrol, Costessey, 1926.

Rover Moot, Birmingham, 1928. Neville Coe (left back), Glaxo, Ted, Yicky, Jack, Jill, Bub and Flop.

Rovers sailing on Ripple III, June 1928.

at their destination, Yorks Wood Park, at 6pm the following day.

A Rover in the 1930s, John Bracey, recalls making a journey in the war canoe on the River Yare. They went from Old Lakenham

One of the first female Venture Scouts to be invested into the Group, Kate Dulieu is pictured with Scout Neil Grogutt, left, and Venture Leader, Derek Page, right, c1982.

Ventures depart for Snowdonia, Wales. March, 1970.

Ripple III, June 1928.

Hall to Bramerton Woods where they camped the night. On the way, the canoe had to be taken out of the water at Trowse and portage made to a haulage yard where they regained access to the river.

Ventures

Venture Scouts for 16 to 20 year olds, replaced Rover Scouts in 1967. At the same time the Baden-Powell Scout Guild was set up to cater for those over 21. From then on, there were few changes until 1976, when the Scout Association made the controversial decision to allow girls to join. In 1981 Kathryn Dulieu and Sam Page were the first girls to be invested as 1st Norwich Venture Scouts.

For thirty-five years succeeding groups of 1st Norwich Ventures followed a busy programme of activities and camping. There were lean times when numbers were low or Leaders were scarce (for a while in 1978 there were only three Ventures), but even then, they made good use of their time by assisting the Scouts and helping with boat maintenance.

Before the present Headquarters was built the Ventures had a Den above a toilet block outside the main building. In it they had armchairs, a television and a record player although, to move around, they had to climb over the tie-bar that was holding the roof together across the middle of the room.

In March 1970, when nine Venture Scouts with Leader Dave Reyner went climbing in Snowdonia, they had to negotiate three-inch deep snow to get to their camp at Llyn Ogwen. In spite of a gale that blew for two days, they managed to climb Mount Tryfan without mishap, reporting that they thoroughly enjoyed the experience.

Charles Bartram (now the Cub Akela), recalls that in the same year they went to France in a minibus. It broke down in Paris before they finally made it to southern France where they had arranged to meet up with some German Scouts.

Other activities of the 1970s included decorating hospital wards at Christmas and contributing to Scout funds by acquiring a marquee and renting it out.

Throughout the 1980s Ventures continued to help with Scout activities. They manned bases at the night hike, 'Shotsilva'. Kathryn Dulieu remembers being *declared dead* by a young Scout at one of the bases where they staged a First Aid incident. She also tells of swimming in the river at Headquarters in winter and having to break the ice to enter the water.

The 1990s was a successful decade for the Venture Unit and in 1997 it was the largest in the District with twelve members. That year they won the Dragon Boat trophy at Whitlingham Regatta, worked as staff at the Welsh Jamboree,

Ventures decorate a Ward at the Norfolk and Norwich Hospital. December, 1977.

Right: Ventures at Headquarters, c1977. Left to right. Back row: Leslie Hill, Venture Leader, Eddy Goldsmith; Martin Thouless. Front row: John Poynter and Richard Goodrum.

Left and above: At the University of East Anglia, 1977

Ventures at Decoy Broad dyke. Easter, 1977.

and individually achieved two Venture Scout Awards and a Queen's Scout Award.

The Ventures took part in many District events. They organised a District camp at 1st Norwich Headquarters in 1994 and a dry-slope skiing event in 1995. In 1999 they organised the canoeing for the Norfolk Jamboree.

They raised money for funds and for charity by completing a sponsored challenge with the Rangers in 1995, where the objective was to travel one hundred miles by as many means as possible. They joined the Scouts walking in the

The Venture Scout team, Baden-Powell Anniversary hike, 1982.

Addy carries out an investiture during a 'mock climbing' event, 1992.

Sheffield area and at Summer Camp in South Wales in 1996 and ran a Christmas party for Scouts and their friends. In addition they went climbing, canoeing and canoe surfing, took part in a two-week self-defence course and came third in the County Venture quiz.

At Headquarters. December, 1992. Left to right. Back row: Donald Stapleton, Venture Leader Derek Page, Maria Hydon, Dominic Kaines. Front row: Stewart Adcock, Jamie Clarke, Chris Smith.

In 1998 they attended the Sherwood Jamboree with Ventures from Leeds and organised a camp at Decoy for older Scouts and Ventures to which a Leeds contingent came.

Ventures have always enjoyed conducting their investitures in unusual circumstances. Four were invested at the Group's 75th Anniversary Service in 1983 and, in 1995, Katie Adcock and others were invested under the blades of a helicopter at the Norfolk Jamboree.

The Vermin Explorer Scout Unit
In 2002, in order to meet changing needs, Venture Units changed to Explorer Units, catering for a

Investiture underneath the blades of a helicopter. July 1995. Left to right: Ellen Green; Sarah Ainsworth; James Ambrozevich; Katie Adcock; James Clements; Flag Bearer, Stewart Adcock; Venture Leader, Derek Page.

younger age group of 14 to 18 year olds.

The 1st Norwich Venture Unit (the Vermin) changed to become the Vermin Explorer Scout Unit. They are now part of Southern Norwich District Explorers and members wear a District scarf, although they are still attached to the 1st Norwich Group. This change in organisation enables Explorer Scouts to work with others in the District and take part in a wider range of activities.

At the Welsh Jamboree, 1997. GSL Alan Adcock (back row, second right), Venture Leader Jill Austin (front left).

Canoe Polo Trophy winners. March 1999. Back row: Danny Willcox, Mike Hoy, Neil Grogutt, James Clements, Julien Pike. Front row: James Ambrozevich, Aaron Bargewell, Paul Beldon, Mark Ambrozevich, Chris Smith.

Chelmsford in July. Earlier, at Easter, they had joined the rest of the contingent on a five-day trip to Luxembourg. There they went sightseeing, climbed hills, sampled the chocolate, and made preparations for the Jamboree.

Vermin Explorers have taken part in a variety of activities such as debating, drama, cooking, firelighting and kayaking. They have run evenings for Scouts, planned Scout night hikes and helped with fundraising. They have also taken part in activities organised by other Explorer Units.

Baden-Powell Anniversary Hike
In 2004 the Vermin Explorer team were the winners of the Baden-Powell Anniversary Hike, an event held to commemorate the birthday in February of the founder of Scouting. It is a County competition, consisting of an all-night

In their first year the Vermin Explorers took up several challenges. They 'Beat the Sun' in a walk along the North Norfolk coast starting at dawn and walking until sunset. They completed a forty-seven mile hike carrying full kit and sleeping overnight in a bunk-house, and they climbed the equivalent height of Mount Everest on the climbing wall. This involved ascending the wall thirteen hundred times in a thirty-six hour period.

Since then, they have travelled to Kandersteg International Scout Centre in Switzerland twice, once in 2003 and again in 2005, with a party of Scouts, when severe floods devastated the area.

Explorers took part in the celebrations for the Centenary of Scouting in 2007. Seven were members of the contingent representing Norfolk at the 21st World Jamboree at Hylands Park,

Vermin Explorers completing the Mount Everest challenge at HQ, 2005.

hike (often in bad weather) of around twelve miles with full packs. At bases along the course teams carry out various Scouting activities and are scored on their performance. The Explorers won by 400 points and were the only team to complete the course.

1st Norwich teams have taken part in the hike regularly over the years with varying degrees of success - once in the 1970s, the Venture team was handicapped after being dropped off at the wrong starting point and, later in 1992, they were awarded a trophy with a boot on it for being the best newcomers.

Ever since their inception, 1st Norwich Rovers, Ventures and Explorers have attended many Jamborees and camped in several different countries. They have taken part in a wide variety of events and always had lots of fun. Explorers now meet weekly at 1st Norwich Headquarters and have a full programme planned for 2008.

Vermin Explorers rifle shooting, 2006.

Fire lighting, 2006.

Three 1st Norwich Explorers, wearing the uniform of the United Kingdom contingent for the 21st World Scout Jamboree, carried the flags for the Norfolk County Centenary of Scouting Service at Norwich Cathedral, June 2007. Left to right: Alex Saunders, Josee Tisdale, Mark Robertson.

Entrants in the District cooking competition, 2006.

Switzerland 2005

In August 2005 a party of twenty-two Scouts and Explorers with three Leaders, went on a nine-day trip to the Kandersteg International Scout Centre in Switzerland. They went by coach, travelling through the night and arriving late on the second day. At the site was a large log cabin and enclosure where they could get together, have fires and cook. Behind this was an area for the tents. It was wet on arrival so they chose to use tents already on site only putting up their large tent to use for meals.

The next day they completed a steep hike to the Glacier Lake in the mountains. The rain

The contingent for Kandersteg, 2005. Explorer Leaders: Danny Willcox, Helen Grogutt and Shaun Culling. Explorers: Paul Robertson, Robbie Wincup, Will Saunders, Luke Cubbage, Will Walker, Sophia Wincup, David Hague, Abbie Robinson and Nikki Bensted-Smith. Scouts: Alex Saunders, Mark Robertson, Sam Penny, Ashley Mitchell, Ryan Mills, Milan Kier-Palmer, Frank Sheppard, Oliver Hendry, Alex and Lizzie Lloyd-Wickens, Jessica Goodwin, Libby Kean and Harrison Grogutt.

A wet hike to Glacier Lake.

was so heavy it soaked through many of their waterproof coats, yet, in spite of the cold, Paul and Big Will stripped off and swam in the lake. Afterwards, everyone warmed up in the café.

By the fourth day the camp was flooded and the large tent had collapsed with the weight of the water. Explorers and Scouts spent the morning sorting out the camp. They lit a fire to keep warm, spread branches over the walkway and dried their gear. While keeping warm around the fire they heard and saw in the distance, the cliffs that form the Kandersteg valley cracking and rockslides forming, … *pouring down the cliff below the clouds and smashing as they fell.* They had

Trying to keep pathways useable at the camp site.

to move into the central building for safety while Switzerland declared a state of emergency due to flash flooding - it had been raining almost non-stop for seventy-two hours.

That night they were able to return to their tents and by the morning it had stopped raining allowing them to enjoy another hike up the mountain to go tobogganing at a dry run.

With a trip to Bern the next day came the realisation of how destructive the weather had been. There were cars floating down roads, water up to the first floor level of houses and

The flooded town of Bern.

helicopters rescuing stranded people and animals. In spite of this they were able to visit the old city, which was on higher ground.

Reflecting on what they had seen, the older Scouts and Explorers volunteered to help. The next day they split up into groups and each was assigned to help a particular family. The work was dirty and sometimes dangerous; they helped

Very muddy Explorers return to camp after helping local residents.

Hurtling down the toboggan shoot.

recover firewood that had been swept away, emptied homes of ruined furniture and pumped out water and dirt from flooded basements.

They were rewarded for their efforts with a free trip to the outdoor swimming pool where they enjoyed swimming in the warm water surrounded by icy mountain caps. A highlight

Their reward is free use of the swimming pool.

Getting ready for the bridge jump.

was the diving-board, which has become a rarity in England. That evening they shared a campfire with friends at the campsite.

The next day they went on a high ropes course, which included bridge jumps, rope swings, scramble nets and high wires. On the last night they began preparations for the trip home having had an experience none could have predicted. In Paul's words they

> … *had shared international experiences and witnessed first hand the devastation caused by natural disaster. It … was an eye-opener in more ways than any one of us could have imagined and to look back we achieved our goal - to live the dream.*

(Summary of Report by Paul Robertson, Vermin ESU)

Descending from the bridge.

Time to reflect.

Beaver Scouts

The Beaver Scout Motto: Fun and Friends

In 1988 the idea of starting a Beaver Section, for six to eight year olds, was put to the 1st Norwich Group Executive Committee as several of the Cubs' younger brothers were keen to join the Scout Movement. The committee agreed and a Beaver Colony was started by Leaders Jane Stafford (nee Blyth) and Glynnis Clements. Twelve Beavers were invested later that year. The standard uniform was a grey sweatshirt and trousers with a turquoise coloured neckerchief. Later this was changed to allow the Beavers to wear the Group neckerchief. The present colour of the sweatshirt is turquoise.

Initially, Beavers were considered by the Scout Association as too young to take part in certain activities such as camping and marching at St George's Day Parades. They were allowed to

The first twelve Beavers invested at Headquarters, March 1988. Back Row: ?, Jane Stafford, Glynnis Clements. Middle Row: Evan Leysham, David Clements, Nicholas Healy, Daniel Monk, Carl Rudd, Jon Boden, Daniel Tink. Front Row: Emmerson Kerr, Shane Whitely, ?, Ashley Cocker, ?.

Performing the Twelve Days of Christmas. December 1988.

Above: St. George's Day Parade, April 1994. Beaver Leaders Elizabeth Culling, left and Ruth Boden, right.

The Group at their 90th Anniversary. Guests included the Lord Mayor and Sheriff of Norwich. Beaver Leader, Sean Quarmby invested Jordon Gott and Spencer Hunt during the Service. January 1998.

line up with the Group for the Lord Mayor's address, but their parents had to take them to the Church for the Service. This rule was later relaxed and today they take part in the full Parade.

Beaver Scouts are now allowed to camp under canvas provided they sleep with their parents and as such took part in the 1998 Group Family Camp at Gt. Hautbois. Sleep-overs are allowed in the Headquarters and, under the Leadership of Joy Parfitt, they held their first one in 2003.

In 2006, the Group decided to follow Scout Association guidelines and allow girls into Beavers, with Chloe Richardson becoming the first female Beaver to be invested in October.

The Beavers work towards achieving various badges, and much of their weekly programme

is planned around this. Joint evenings are arranged with the Cubs for occasions such as the Christmas Show, Easter Egg Hunts and Halloween. Beavers have visited elderly residents at Corton House in City Road at Christmas, taking them gifts they have made.

Under the guidance of their Leader, the Beaver Colony devised their own song. In 2007 the

Cubs and Beavers at Family Camp, 1998. Leaders, left to right: Sean Quarmby, David Driver, Jane Stafford, Charles Bartram, David Albury.

'Fishing for tiddlers' during the first Beaver sleep-over held at Headquarters, August 2003.

Beavers in their turquoise sweaters at Harvest Festival, September 2002. Leaders: Robert Hawes and Joy Parfitt. Beavers left to right: Kieran and Liam Mills, Jordon Newton, Thomas Lingard, Billy Farrow, Jordon Flegg, Owen Cunningham.

Seaside theme at the 2005 sleepover. Beavers, left to right: Charlie Lloyd-Wickens, Dominic Trevor, ?, Joseph Rix, Ross Gilbert, Benedict Armitage, ?, Kyle Richardson, Oliver Truswell, Jack Howard, Milo Butcher.

words of the song were embroidered on a
square included in the Norfolk County Beaver
Banner, which was made as part of the initiative
to commemorate the Centenary of the Scout
Movement.

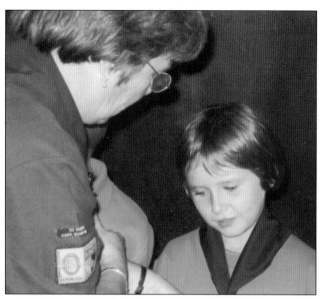

*Beaver Leader Joy Parfitt invests Chloe Richardson, the first girl
to join the Beaver Colony. October 6th, 2006.*

*Chloe Richardson (centre) with other Beavers invested on the
same date. Leaders, left to right: Alison MacNab, Sara Cordy, Joy
Parfitt, Robert Hawes. Beavers, left to right: Ethan Rose, Alex
Koloka, Max Reeve, Charlie Emmerson, Connor Southwell.*

*The Beaver song embroidered on the Norfolk Centenary County
Beaver Banner, 2007.*

*Beavers visit Corton House on City Road, December 2007. Left
to right, back row: Mikey Coleman, William Patient, William
Webster, Alfie Gadd, Charlie Emmerson, Toby Chisnell, Centre
row with residents, Zoe Rickard. Front row: Jude Sutton, Cass
Veal, Joshua Saunders, Isaac Yuill.*

FINGOS: First Norwich Group of Old Scouts

In 1958 a group of ex-Scouts, led by Edward Coe, set up the 1st Norwich Branch of the B-P (Baden-Powell) Scout Guild. They called themselves FINGGOS, an abbreviation of 'First Norwich Group Guild of Old Scouts' and their objective was to stay formally involved in their old Scout Group.

Nineteen years later, in 1977, when Branches of the B-P (Baden-Powell) Scout Guild were officially closed down, the group carried on although with a slightly different title. They adapted their former name, dropping the word 'Guild' to become more simply the First Norwich Group of Old Scouts or FINGOS and this is the name that is commonly recognised today.

Initially there were fifteen members, with the number rising to thirty-nine in the early 1960s when the annual subscription was 10/- (50p) per head. Half of this had to be paid to the national B-P Scout Guild and FINGGOS had problems paying their quota as well as finding money to support the Scout Group, so for a time they joined forces with the Norwich District B-P Guild to hold fundraising events. The Rev. J Mosby DSO (Pilot), who had been involved with the 1st Norwich Scout Group since the early days, was a member and for some time served

FINGOS members gathered for lunch at How Hill, 1988.

The names of those present at the lunch in 1988 alongside the date they first made their Scout Promise.

The Silver Acorn Medal belonging to the Rev J Mosby DSO.

as Chairman. He was awarded the Silver Acorn in 1966 and after his death in 1972 his widow presented it to the Scout Group.

FINGOS members at the Dedication of the new flag, Old Lakenham Parish Church, 1992. Left to right: Scout Carl Newitt, ?, Gordon Hatch, William Barber, Frank Folkard, a Beaver, Basil Craske, Cub Alex Swinbourne.

FINGGOS met regularly and in the early years went hiking and camping together. At their meetings they were kept up to date with the welfare of the Scout Group by the Group Scout Master; Skipper Greenfield at first, then later Addy Adcock. The help they gave to the Scouts was invaluable. They assisted at St. George's Day Parades, organised the embroidery of scarves and badges, and worked on the maintenance of Scout Headquarters. In the 1970s they painted the outside and helped with repairs. Special thanks were given to Frank Folkard (Nunky) for

83

1st Norwich neckerchief belonging to Frank Folkard depicting the Deep Sea Scout emblem along with his Deep Sea Scout badge attached to a wrist strap.

his work on the quay heading. (Nunky has been a member of the Group since the 1930s and, while in the Royal Navy during the Second World War, he joined the Deep Sea Scouts. These Scouts, who served on ships, could take advantage of worldwide contacts in order to continue Scouting activities while away from home.

To commemorate the 60th Anniversary of the 1st Norwich Scout Group, FINGGOS presented them with a wooden engraved plaque, bearing the inscription "1st Norwich Scouts Diamond Jubilee".

The President's chair presented to the Group in 1967 in memory of Skipper Coe.

On the death of Edward Coe in February 1964, the remaining FINGGOS set up a memorial fund. Over £200 was raised and used to commission a President's chair, benches and a wooden record chest for the Court of Honour. These were presented at the official opening of the new Headquarters in 1967.

Skipper Coe's ashes were buried under the Altar that stood in the grounds of Old Lakenham Hall, an area known as 'The Chapel'. It was well looked after by his widow, Maidie, and members of FINGGOS who in 1968 made good the paved area and planted flower beds.

When Old Lakenham Hall was sold, discussions took place as to what was to happen to the Altar. FINGGOS and other members of the 1st Norwich

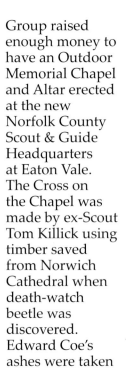

The inscription on the President's chair.

Plaque presented to the Group on its 60th anniversary in 1968.

Group raised enough money to have an Outdoor Memorial Chapel and Altar erected at the new Norfolk County Scout & Guide Headquarters at Eaton Vale. The Cross on the Chapel was made by ex-Scout Tom Killick using timber saved from Norwich Cathedral when death-watch beetle was discovered. Edward Coe's ashes were taken from Old Lakenham Hall and placed beneath the chapel floor at Eaton Vale. The Chapel was officially handed over to the County Association on October 23rd 1979 and when Edward's son Colonel Mark Coe MBE was killed in 1980, whilst serving in Germany, his ashes were placed near those of his father.

In September 1982, Mrs Maidie Coe planted a Ginkgo tree nearby to commemorate the 1st Norwich Group's 75th Anniversary.

The group, which had continued to exist after the changes of 1977 when they altered their name to FINGOS, were still getting together for an annual luncheon with their wives in the early 1990s. At the present time however, it is inactive although there are still many ex-Scouts who keep in contact and give support to the 1st Norwich Scout Group. Hopefully a new generation of 'Old Scouts' will revive FINGOS to ensure our present members have guidance from the past members.

Altar in the outdoor Chapel at Old Lakenham Hall.

Above: FINGOS members at the Edward Coe Chapel.
Mrs Maidie Coe seated, centre.

Right: The Edward Coe Chapel at Eaton Vale.

Mrs Maidie Coe plants a
ginko tree at Eaton vale,
1982.

Camps, Rallies and Jamborees 1919-1939

Camps were held at many different sites in Norfolk, often on land made available by local landowners who were involved in the Scout Movement. Favourite places for summer and weekend camps were Benacre Denes near Lowestoft, Taverham Mill, Quidenham Hall, Costessey Hall, Happisburgh and Eccles. The Scouts also took in rallies and other events organised by the District and County Boy Scout Associations where, on several occasions, they were privileged to meet Sir Robert Baden-Powell and members of the Royal Family. They also travelled further afield to attend national and international camps and World Jamborees.

HRH Prince Henry, Duke of Gloucester inspecting the Guard of Honour at the Norwich Association Rally, Crown Point, 1922. (The venue for rallies held in 1914 and 1920.)

Scouts with the trek cart at the District Rally. City of Norwich School, 1919.

Lunch during a visit to the Tower of London on the occasion of the Imperial Jamboree at Wembley, 1924.

Camping at Benacre Denes

The Scouts first camped at Benacre in 1913 and, from 1919, returned every summer for five years. In 1920 the newly formed Rover Patrol helped out by guarding the stores at night and walking eight miles each day to fetch bread and meat from Kessingland. Equipment was transported by lorry and trek cart, but not always without mishap. A Scout pulling a trek cart by bicycle had an accident and, once, the lorry got stuck in the sand when they were leaving for home. Activities at camp included signalling, patrol relay races, camp-fires, cooking, concerts and Soc-Rugger, a cross between football and rugby invented by the Troop in 1911.

In 1921 they took the Cubs to camp but the responsibility of looking after them, especially when their tent blew down in the night, led to a decision not to take them again.

A dip in the ocean, 1922.

Transport to camp: Above, 1921. Below, 1923, on the corner of Glebe Road and Jessop Road.

Benacre denes, 1923. View of the camp, above.
Patrol at dinner, right.

Norfolk County Rally, Mousehold Aerodrome, Norwich 1926

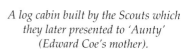

A log cabin built by the Scouts which
they later presented to 'Aunty'
(Edward Coe's mother).

Edward Coe mounts the podium (above) to address the Rally
(right) 1926.

Above: A rope bridge over the pond. One of the many displays and
demonstrations given by the Scouts.

Right: Edward Coe (left) with the Chief Scout (centre), 1926.

Camps at Taverham

Camps held at Taverham in the 1920s and 30s included Leaders' training camps. Regular events included ditch-jumping, climbing trees, bathing at the meadow, cutting nettles and practising axemanship. A high trek cart with iron-shod wheels was taken to camp by cyclists, who often fell off going downhill when the traces caught round the bicycle wheels.

Camp at Taverham Mill, 1924.

'Tex Mac Coe' (Neville Coe) rope spinning, 1922.

Left: Ditch jumping on the common at Taverham, 1929.

Right: Axemanship, 1931.

Norwich Scout Circus 1928

Held in Ipswich Road, the Scout Circus was a day of displays, trek cart races and entertainments. The 1st Norwich Troop were involved in a Grand Parade of Prehistoric Animals. (They had taken part in a similar display at Alexandra Palace, London in 1922.) They also gave a rodeo display, which included rope-spinning and stock-whip cracking.

Rope spinners entering the arena. Left to right: Curley, Sambo, Sticks, Paddy, Felix, Mike and Bunny spinning the rope, 1923.

Trek cart race at the Scout Circus. 1st Norwich team gets away, 1928.

Summer Camps at Happisburgh and Eccles

The campsite at Happisburgh, 1926.

Stags' gateway. Summer camp, Happisburgh, 1926.

Patrol dining shelter, Happisburgh, 1926.

Morning Parade, Eccles, 1927.

Climbing in the sand dunes, Eccles, 1930.

Jamboree, Salhouse Broad Farm, 7th to 9th June, 1930

VIP guests on the podium. The Chief Scout Baden-Powell (left), who was present for the opening camp-fire and HRH Prince George, who attended the Wolf Cub Rally held the next day. On the far left is Lord Playfair, Commissioner for Suffolk and far right Lord Albermarle.

Sea Scouts in canoes with the flying boat on the Broad at the Salhouse Jamboree. They gave displays on the Broad, put on a sketch at the camp-fire, built a Zulu Kraal and made an Indian rope bridge.

The 1st Norwich camp was a mock-up of a Zulu Kraal.

View of the Jamboree arena.

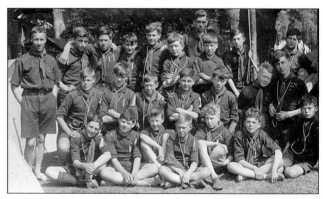

The Troop under 'Sub' (W Barber) at the Salhouse Jamboree.

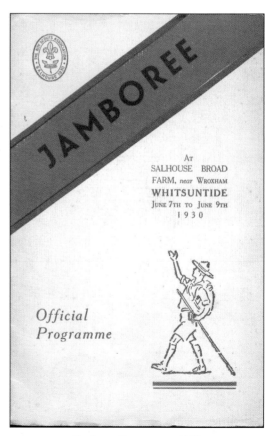

Jamboree Programme 1930

Camps at Costessey

Left: Camp at Costessey Hall, c1924.

Right: Rover Patrol kitchen, 1926.

1st Norwich Gateway, at the Costessey Jamboree, 1934.

Edward Coe with HRH Prince George at the Costessey Jamboree, 1934.

The windmill gateway to the Norfolk camp at the Costessey Jamboree, 1934. It was later re-erected in the grounds of Old Lakenham Hall.

Camping at Quidenham

During the 1920s and 1930s camps were held at Quidenham Hall, which was the home of Lord Albemarle, who was the Norfolk County Commissioner for Scouts.

The canteen tent, 1924.

Playing French cricket, 1925.

Making a noise at tea-time, 1924.

The diving stage on the mere at Quidenham, 1928.

An account of Summer Camp 1933

We have an account of the summer camp in 1933 when Scouts were joined by some of the 1st Thetford Troop and Teddy Wolski, a visitor from Poland. It tells of how they played soc-rugger, tip-and-run cricket, rounders and 'arrow slinging'. They went exploring, lost a game of cricket to the local village team and played a stalking game using semaphore. They swam and took boats out on the mere, having earlier rebuilt a diving stage and fixed up a telephone line from there to the main store tent. There was a night game attacking a fort and a 'blanketeer movement' where Scouts ran through camp in blankets. An obstacle course was set up which involved climbing a tree by hoisting each other up using staves, axemanship in the woods, constructing a bridge and rowing to the middle of the mere then using a 'bivvy sheet' as a sail to get to the other side.

Rowing on the mere, 1931.

Younger boys were taken out on the water, thus fuelling their wish to be Sea Scouts.

Patrols were judged daily on sanitation, punctuality, cooking, and campfire. Beads were awarded and placed on a knitting needle mounted on a broom handle in the camp. Different colours denoted plus and minus marks which were totalled at the end of the day. Seagulls won the competition overall and Stags won a shield for the best camp-fire entertainment.

The camp flagstaff had a top-mast, yard-arm and lateral stays. The Scout pennant flew at the top-mast, the Union Jack at the yard and, at one end of the stay, flew a flag bearing the colours of the winning patrol.

A visitors' day was held and several carloads of parents came. On another day an unexpected visit from Lady Albemarle saw Scouts rushing to get properly dressed when they heard her car coming.

When it rained the camp-fire was held in a large square tent.

There were two casualties. Chink fell on a spade and split his buttock and Chuckle broke his nose playing soc-rugger. Both were taken to hospital before being sent home. Chuckle surprised everyone by returning on his bicycle a few days later.

At the end of camp, the Troop … *manned the drags attached to the chariot wheels* and pulled the boats from the mere up to the beech tree near the track ready for transport back to Wroxham.

The American Jamboree, Washington 1937

Patrol Leader Basil Craske (front row, second from right) was chosen to lead the British Sea Scout Patrol at the American Jamboree, Washington, 1937.

Scouts at Camp and on the Water, 1950-2008

The Scout and Guide Rally, Keswick, Norfolk, 1951.
Above: In the arena with the Loch Ness Monster.
Right: Gateway to the 1st Norwich camp.

Boys and equipment on the way to camp. c1950.

The 1st Norwich Troop at the Coronation Jamboree. Sandringham, 1953.
Leaders, Basil Craske (left), Eric Greenfield (3rd from right) and Frank Folkard.
(right).

Right: Launching canoes at the Taverham Jamboree, 1961.
French and German Scouts joined the 1st Norwich camp at Taverham Mill.

Some who were there remember leaving camp at night and canoeing up-river to a sub camp, narrowly missing discovery on their return at sunrise. On one night, some of the German Scouts went with them and travelled back by bike, crashing on the way.

*The Troop at the Sandringham Jamboree, 1964.
GSL Eric Greenfield in white.*

Stilt tower. Sandringham Jamboree, 1964.

*At the National Sea Scout Regatta, Longridge c1976.
Leaders: Alan Adcock (left), Dave Reyner (right).*

*Leander Sea Scout headquarters, Kingston-on-Thames. Site of the
National Sea Scout Regatta, 1977.*

Martin Thouless and Leslie Hill rowing, 1977.

"IT CAN BE DONE"

At a camp at Lake Bassenthwaite in the early 1980s, the Scout Leader at the time, Derek Page, remembers one morning ... *with the smell of bacon and eggs, wood smoke and coffee drifting through the woods.* He was taking some time to himself in one of the toilet tents when the RAF decided to practise low flying on full after-burn just fifty feet from the tent. At the same camp he hooked and lost a large pike and put everyone off going into the water to swim or wash.

He tells of two Patrol Leaders who went sailing, both with the idea of rolling out of the boat and swimming ashore, leaving the other boy in the boat. Their timing was ... *so perfect that neither knew the other had also rolled out.* They swam at least fifty yards before they noticed, to their surprise, the boat had turned and was following at speed. He had never seen two boys swim so fast.

When they camped at Rudyard Lake in Staffordshire, the lake dried out leaving a very fine, slimy mud. Scouts had to cross the mud to collect water from a spring on the other side, leaving him to work out how to clean over thirty boys and girls with a very limited water supply. His solution was to invent an active game in long grass before tea each day.

Derek also recalls how the Troop was so good at First Aid that, when they staged a van accident simulation, a passing motorist reported witnessing an accident and called an ambulance.

On a hike. Lake Bassenthwaite, early 1980s.

An outboard motor found in the mud at Rudyard Lake in the early 1980s.

Camp cooking at Decoy Broad, c1980. Centre, Neil Grogutt. Right, Paul Davies.

Trophy winners, Whitlingham Regatta, 1984. Left to right: Neil Grogutt, Alistair Pike, Donald Stapleton.

Above and right: Rafting and rowing on Decoy Broad, 1982.

An icy Easter Camp, c1983.

Derek Page (right of centre) with Scouts on Pooh Bear, 1983.

*Peter Newbery Trophy winners, 1984.
Leaders: Alan Adcock, left and Dave
Walford, right.*

Summer Camp, Decoy Broad, Woodbastwick 1986.

Investing a new Scout.
Leaders: Derek Page (left), Alan Adcock (second left).

Danny Willcox and Stewart Adcock, Kayaking.

The Mirror dinghy and kayaks on the Broad.

Lining up for a photocall.

Rowing.

Left: Stag Patrol ready for inspection. Left to right: Stewart Adcock, Andrew Watts, Ian Blackburn, Philip Woods, ?, David Albury.

James Clements, Whitlingham Regatta, 1989.

Stephen Cornwall climbing in Derbyshire, 1990.

Julien Pike leads a campfire song, 1991.

Scouts on the MTB 102, 1990. Ben Parfitt, front row 2nd left. His grandfather served on this boat during WWII.

The 470 sailing boat on Decoy Broad, 1990. It was twenty-five years old when it was sold in 1996.

In the Lake District, 1992.

Katie Adcock (left) and Clare Boden. Decoy Broad, 1993.

*Sleeping out at summer camp in the Lake District, 1992.
Left to right: Daniel Tink, Jon Boden, Aaron Bargewell, Daniel
Perry.*

Campfire at the Family Camp, 1998.

*Scouts on Family Camp,
1998.
Leaders (back row, from
left): Neil Grogutt with baby
Harrison, Danny Wilcox,
Julian Greenfield, Katie
Adcock, Alan Adcock.*

Left: 1st Norwich Leaders with the Chief Scout, George Purdy (centre), at the Norfolk Jamboree, 1999. Julien Pike (left), Jane Stafford (third from left), Joy Parfitt (far right) next to Andrew Cooke.

Right: Covered in mud. Silver Cross camp site. South Wales, 2003.

Backwoods cooking, 2004.

Above and below right: Water activities, 2004.

Top: Wet and happy, 2004 (left); Bell boats, 2004 (right).
Centre: Abseiling.
Bottom: Archery, Easter 2005 (left); Girls at camp, 2005 (right).

Above: On the water, 2005.
Right: On an aerial runway. From left: Jordan Palmer,
Sam Penny and Paul Robertson.

Climbing, 2005.

Camp fire.

Cross country cycling, Easter camp, 2005.

Baking, 2005.

Far left: Lizzie Lloyd-Wickens gets a Special Achievement award, 2006.

Centre: Crate stacking, 2006.

Above: Firelighting. Harrison Grogutt, 2007.

Summer camp, Swansea, 2007.
Above left: Covered in mud.

Above: Obstacle course. Source of the mud.

Left: On the Beach. Left to right at back: Milan Palmer, ASL Katie Adcock, SL Julian Greenfield, Declan Burton, Dean Ward, Jake Reeve, Shaun Culling. Kneeling: Andrew Elliot, Alex Wood.

Cubs at Camp

In 1921 the Scouts took twelve Cubs to summer camp at Benacre Denes. They enjoyed the camp but as Skipper Coe reported, the leaders found looking after them hard work.

Cubs at Benacre camp, 1921.

Cleaning the oiled sea-bird found by the Cubs at Benacre, 1921.

One night the wind rose and swept across The Denes from the north. The bell tent containing the Cubs collapsed and we … *dashed out with large pegs with which we anchored the tent against the wind. Two hours later the wind* changed and blew … *from the opposite direction. Out we went again, with more pegs.* The Cubs … *thoroughly enjoyed the thrills.*

T W Killick, who was a Cub at the time, remembered Fuzz Spalding … *being ticked off by Mr Coe, for chasing somebody's goats.* Also during the camp the cubs rescued a tarred 'sea-bird' which the scouts looked after and cleaned.

At the end of the camp the Scouts decided that the responsibility had been too great and they made a decision not to take the Cubs camping again. The Cubs were however allowed to visit the Scouts at camps and jamborees and take part in activities while they were there.

Visiting the Scout camp at Quidenham Hall, 1925.

Right: Cubs at the Norfolk Jamboree at Salhouse, 1930. They all sat open-mouthed while national hero, Chief Scout Baden-Powell paid a visit to a Zulu Kraal built by the 1st Norwich Rovers. (Alfred Buttle)

Cubs with HRH Prince George at the Costessey Jamboree, 1934.

Cubs with their hobby horses at the Scout and Guide Rally. Keswick, Norfolk, 1951.

Cub Leaders Dinah Higham and Mary Palmer with Cubs at Buckmore Park, Kent, 1958.

At camp at the cricket pavilion. Guist, Norfolk, c1959. Left to right: Peter Lemon, Ian Robson, Jerald Daniels, Peter Mann, David Brown, Andrew Lemon, Paul Downes, Philip Johnson, William Buxton, Paul Lacey, Richard Caceston. A story is told of one 'accident prone' Cub who knocked over the stove and set fire to the pavilion. The same Cub also hit his head when he decided to use an axe for cutting rhubarb.

At camp at Budleigh Salterton, 1962. The young Cub in the centre is Charles Bartram.

Left: Cubs at camp at Eaton Vale, 1987. During the 1970s and 1980s, Cubs attended several District Camps at Eaton Vale, went to the County Rally at RAF Marham (1971) and made visits to Decoy Broad.

Camping at Trimingham, Norfolk 1988 – 2003

Right: Transport to camp, 1988. Standing, left to right: Jenny Smith, Jane Stafford, Mick and Glynnis Clements, Roy Bargewell, Val Bargewell, Charles Bartram, Joy Parfitt, Graham Fuller, Emma Bartram, Mandy Ansell. Kneeling at front, Alan Blyth. The four day camp led by Jane Stafford (formerly Blyth) and Charles Bartram with support from parents, was the first of several annual camps held at Trimingham. The 1950s coach was loaned by Mr Ernie Green and driven by parent, Mr Mick Clements. It had a cruising speed of only 30mph, which led to a local traffic alert on the radio advising drivers of a slow-moving vehicle causing severe tail-backs on the Norwich to North Walsham road.

Left: On a hike from camp at Trimingham, 1988.

Below: The 'Sir Walter Raleigh' team at Trimingham camp, 1993. Parent helpers, Dave Swinbourne and Jane Wincup.

'Taking a rest' on the camp hike. Mundesley, 1994.

Jane Stafford with newly invested Cubs. Trimingham, 1994. Left to right: James Swinbourne, Jonathan Fletcher, Shaun Culling, Christopher Wincup.

Charles invests Scott and Lee at Trimingham Camp, 1997.

Catching crabs on Mundesley beach, 1996.

Trimingham camp, 2003. Adults, left to right: Gavin Rix, Valerie White, Charles Bartram, Claire Lloyd-Wickens, Chris Regan, David Albury, Shaun Culling, Francis Taylor. Scout helper, front right, Will Saunders.

Below: Crabbing at Blakeney, 2003.

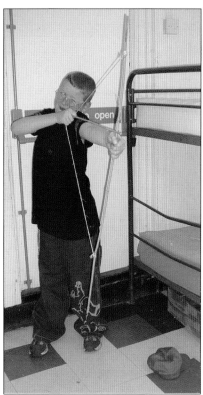

Alex Lloyd-Wickens with his hand made bow, 2003.

Time for games. Trimingham, 2003.

Camping at Wells-Next-The-Sea 1996

In 1996 the Cub summer camp was held at the Sea Scout Headquarters, Wells-on-Sea. Gale force winds on the first day meant that they had to camp indoors. The Headquarters was divided into sections for sleeping, with the adults in their hike tents and the cubs on the floor. Before settling down for the evening the Cubs walked single-file along the Harbour front where, alarmingly, the high tides and strong winds caused the water to lap over the sides of the harbour. They sought shelter for a couple of hours in the Amusement Arcade or 'Electric House' as one Cub called it, each cub having 50 pence to spend. The next day the wind had lessened and they were able to erect the tents outside.

Crabbing at Wells Harbour.

Wells camp, 1996. Adults, left to right: Keith and Jane Wincup, Clare Brett, Sue Hunton, ?, Charles Bartram, Patrick Smith, David Albury, Mike Hunton, David Culling, Jane Stafford.

Setting off on a trip to see the seals. Morston.

Busy at camp. Wells.

Father and Son Camps

Cubs and their fathers at camp. 1st Norwich headquarters, 1994. Adults, left to right: David Culling, Richard Godfrey, Keith Denham, Dave Swinbourne,?, Mike Hunton. Father and son, and family camps have provided opportunities for parents, many who have never camped before, to join their children in activity packed weekends.

Father and son camp. 1st Norwich headquarters, 1997. Leaders and parents, standing, left to right: Jane Stafford, David Albury, Sean Quarmby, Keith Wincup, Joy Parfitt, Michael Brett, David Culling, Charles Bartram.

Family Camp, Great Hautbois 1998

Above, and right: Cubs and Beavers enjoying a Family camp at Great Hautbois, Norfolk. 1998.

District Camps and Camps at Headquarters

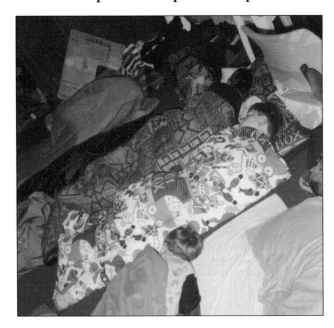

Above: A sleepover at 1ˢᵗ Norwich headquarters at the first District Cub Night Hike, 1996.

Above right: Charles entertains the Pack, 1998.

Right: Rafting at District camp, 2003.

The team competing in the District cooking competition. District camp, Eaton Vale, 2006.

Feeding the ducklings at summer camp. 1ˢᵗ Norwich headquarters, 2007. Young Helper Tom Egleton, centre.

World Jamborees

After its formation, the Scout Movement quickly spread to many other countries and Baden-Powell soon had plans to hold an international gathering of Scouts. However, because of the advent of the First World War, this did not come about until 1920, when the first World Jamboree was held in London. Since then, a World Jamboree has been held every fourth year, except during the Second World War.

The 1st Norwich Troop sent representatives to most of the World Jamborees until 1957. They were represented again in 2007, the centenary year of the Scout Movement, when seven Explorer Scouts were part of the Norfolk Contingent at the 21st World Jamboree at Hylands Park, Chelmsford in Essex.

1st World Jamboree 1920, Olympia.
Eleven First Class Scouts went by train to the Jamboree at Olympia. They camped at Richmond Park, visited the Jamboree and went sight-seeing.

The Troop at Richmond Park, 1920.

3rd World Jamboree 1929, Arrowe Park, Birkenhead.
The trip to the Jamboree was combined with a camping tour in a hired bus. En route to Liverpool the Scouts camped at Matlock and Chester and after the Jamboree they toured Wales, visiting Mount Snowdon, Barmouth, Brecknock and Monmouth. Each Scout paid £3 and, in addition, had to have a certificate to say that he was free from infectious disease, which was a requirement of the Jamboree authority. Bert Batch (Shrimp), remembered the good time they all had, especially having to uproot a gate-post to get the bus into a field, the driver's quick reaction when the engine caught fire, and wrestling while covered with margarine.

4th World Jamboree 1933, Hungary.
1st Norwich were represented at the Jamboree, in Godollo.

Indian Scouts who attended the 3rd World Jamboree, on a visit to Norwich, 1929.

En route to the 3rd World Jamboree, 1929.

Scouts with the coach hired for the camping tour, 1929.

5th World Jamboree 1937, Vogelenzang, Holland.

Eric Greenfield and P Peeke travelled to the two-week Jamboree held in August. They met Scouts from many other countries, played in the mouth organ band, for which they got much applause, and took part in a march-past in the presence of the Chief Scout and Queen Wilhelmina. They went sightseeing by train and boat before returning to Norwich having had … *a fine holiday.*

6th World Jamboree 1947, Jamboree of Peace, France

Group Scout Master John Seymour represented the Troop and was in charge of the Norfolk contingent of Scouts.

Michael Palmer and Julian O'Dell underneath the Norfolk windmill gateway at the 9th World Jamboree, 1957.

Philip, the Prime Minister Harold Macmillan and the Chief Scout Lord Rowallan.

21st World Jamboree July 2007, Hylands Park, Chelmsford, Essex.

Seven 1st Norwich Explorers joined Iceni Troop, one of the two Troops making up the eighty-strong Norfolk contingent at the 21st World Jamboree. Members of Iceni Troop already knew each other, having made a five-day visit to Wiltz in Luxembourg at Easter in preparation for the event. Two 1st Norwich Leaders also attended as part of the International Service Team.

There were over 40,000 Scouts from 180 different countries at the Jamboree, which took the theme One World – One Promise, a

Queen's Scout Peter Gibb (right) with Ian Aitchison from the 22nd Norwich and Rupert Crisp from the 30th Norwich on their way to the 8th World Jamboree in Canada, 1955.

8th World Jamboree 1955, Niagara-on-the-Lake, Canada.

Peter Gibb travelled to Canada with two other Norfolk Sea Scouts having qualified to join the English contingent by gaining his Queen's Scout badge

9th World Jamboree 1957, Sutton Coldfield.

1st Norwich Scouts Michael Palmer (Squeak) and Julian O'Dell (Caesar) went to the Jamboree, which was attended by 35,000 Scouts from 84 different countries. Visitors to the Jamboree included Her Majesty Queen Elizabeth and Prince

'Iceni' Troop representing Norfolk at the 21st World Scout Jamboree, 2007.

'Iceni' Troop in Luxembourg, Easter 2007.

45,000 people took part in the Ceremony, linked by satellite to Brownsea Island, the site of Baden-Powell's first Scout camp. The Explorers found it a moving Ceremony, which highlighted the challenges facing the world and how the biggest youth movement of all time can make a difference.

In his account of the Jamboree, Explorer Mark Robertson says it was

… an experience of a lifetime … it was heart-moving and emotional … we were able to explore different cultures … and make new friends …

reminder of the Scout Law which is common to all Scouts and by which they all live.

The opening ceremony, attended by His Royal Highness Prince William and His Royal Highness the Duke of Kent, on 28th July, was followed by two weeks of action and adventure. There were many activities available, which included the opportunity to make friends, learn about other cultures and to sample food from other countries. Among other things, the Explorers went climbing, abseiling, took part in water activities and worked on a local community project.

On 1st August at 8.00am local time, Scouts all around the world renewed their Promise at a Sunrise Ceremony to mark the start of the second century of Scouting. At Hylands Park, an estimated

Richard Butler, Norfolk County Commissioner (centre in pink), meets some of the Norfolk contingent at the Jamboree.

It has changed our lives and how we look at different issues … and (showed us) how we can help around the world … Scouting has lasted 100 years, it's up to us to take it through the next 100 years.

1st Norwich Explorers help to build the windmill gateway on their sub-camp.

Scouts proudly display the English and Jamboree flags.

1st Norwich Leaders Joy Parfitt (left) and Jane Stafford (right), members of the International Service Team, meet the Chief Scout, Peter Duncan.

Right: Badges from Jamborees attended by the Troop until 1957, displayed on the original Troop flag.

Far Right: Badges, including the official badge of the 21st World Scout Jamboree, displayed on the Group flag made in 1991.

Hiking, Climbing, Orienteering and more . . .

As Scouting has changed with the times, so have many of the activities undertaken by Scouts who now have access to technology not even dreamed about earlier. Basic Scouting, however, has not changed, although the facilities and equipment used may be different. Scouts still go hiking and climbing, play games, entertain and contribute to the community. Some of the activities undertaken by the 1st Norwich over its hundred-year history are illustrated here.

Hiking

Hiking has always been a popular and essential activity for Scouts. In the early days walking was a common means of everyday transport and completion of a three-day hike was a requirement for the First Class badge. Scouts would often walk miles to get to a campsite sometimes pulling trek-carts laden with gear. They were encouraged to draw maps and make observations of the route as they walked and night hikes were used to develop the ability to find their way in the dark.

At Easter in 1924, two Scouts, 'Bunny' High and Jill Roberts, set out on a three-day hike. They were to meet up with the rest of the Troop on the third day, when they would all continue by car to Stanmore for the Wembley Jamboree. They walked the first nine miles in good time and camped. The temperature fell below freezing during the night and they woke early to eat hot cross buns and have a cold wash in a bucket under a pump. At their second camp, they met an old gentleman who gave them more eggs and potatoes than they could carry, so the next day they set out with heavy loads. This took a toll on their feet and ended in disaster. ... *alas, our poor feet. We cooled them in a stream by the wayside ... and ... poor Jill's eggs ... all nicely spread over blankets, pyjamas and face flannel!* Jill's feet became covered with *tender cushioned blisters*. He removed his socks and shoes and finished the hike barefoot.

Nowadays walking is less often used purely as a means of transport but Scouts still hike in the countryside, getting close to nature and learning to navigate and survive in the wild. Night hikes are popular and the 1st Norwich annually participate in the District night hike (Night Owl competition), which they have won many times.

Climbing

Scouts have been climbing and abseiling since they built their first climbing tripod at Jessopp Road headquarters in the 1920s. Since then, they have climbed on their own tower at Headquarters, at climbing centres, and when away at camp.

Checking the map. Scouts on a hike with Explorer Leader, Shaun Culling (left), and Assistant Scout Leader, Neil Grogutt (right). Summer camp, Swansea, 2007.

Phlop and Jack, from Kangaroo Patrol, setting out on their First Class hike from Benacre to Covehithe in 1922.

Scouts in front of the climbing tower at Headquarters after taking part in the Everest climbing challenge. May, 1990.

117

Climbing on the tower at Headquarters, c2003.

Pioneering in the Troop room, 1972.

Stags Patrol competing in the Peter Newbery Trophy, 1991.

Building a bridge at camp, c1980.

Orienteering

Orienteering is a sport which involves navigating cross-country by map-reading and using a compass.

Pioneering

Pioneering was one of the earliest of Scouting activities. It requires teamwork and knowledge of knotting and lashing. Poles are lashed together to make towers, bridges, and other structures.

The Peter Newbery Trophy

Teams competed for the Peter Newbery Trophy at an annual District Activity Day held through the late 1980s and the 1990s. The 1st Norwich Group were regular competitors and, in 1988, both the Cubs and the Scouts received trophies. The Trophy was set up by Shirley Newbery in memory of her late husband, Peter, who had been a Cringleford Scout Leader.

1st Norwich Cubs and Scouts receiving the Trophy from Shirley Newbery in 1988.

The 1st Norwich team Orienteering at Horsford Woods c1991. Left to right.
Back row: Hannah Smith, Carl Everitt, Clare Boden, James Ambrozevich,
James Clements, Mark Balls.
Middle row: ?, Paul Storey, Daniel Monk, Jon Boden, Karl Spurdon, Matthew
Storey. Front row: Leaders Danny Wilcox, Ruth Boden, Julien Pike, Jane Stafford.

hand and the weapons had to be confiscated.

Football

A football club was formed in 1912 under Scoutmaster Charles Bower. The game was considered … *splendid training for the eye, brain, wind and muscle.* Scouts were reminded however that … *in this Troop Scout work comes first, not football.* Scouts and Cubs have continued to play football over the years with varying success in competition.

Soc-rugger

Soc-rugger was a game invented at summer camp in 1911. It was described by Charles Bower as a kind of football with handball. It was a rough game … *calculated to restore circulation after the coldest bath and to act as a safety valve when tempers are rising.* Players were not allowed to … *trip, hack, punch or throw opponents.*

Archery

Skipper Coe tells us that archery was first introduced at a camp in the 1920s, using bows made from green wood. Arrows were made from reeds with the points covered with strips of elder wood. He says that marksmanship improved so much that a mug of tea was shattered in his

The Scout five-a-side football team, c1988.

"Students of the Bow," 1924.

Archery at summer camp. Swansea, 2007.

Shin hockey
Shin hockey has been played since the early days of the Troop and is still played today. It is played with a short stick and sometimes a hard cricket ball.

On the air
In 1984 Scouts joined in the Jamboree on the Air. This national event, held annually since 1958, allows Scouts around the world to communicate using amateur radio.

Troop magazines
The first Troop magazine, The Readiscout, was published in 1913. It contained news of the Troop, general information about Scouting, jokes and topical articles. It was replaced by The Hawk in 1920 but publication ceased a year later as it had become too costly. An attempt was made to start up The 1st Norwich Gazette in the 1930s but only one issue was published. Patrols, in the past, have published their own magazines such as the Owler and the Stags magazines of the 1920s.

Playing shin hockey on the beach, 1930.

Parents Paul Turnham and Aleck Bartram, helping at the Jamboree on the Air, 1984.

The cover of the first Troop magazine, Readiscout 1913.

Concerts and Entertainments
The Troop held their first concert in July 1912 and, thereafter, put on a concert in most years until the Second World War. The programme would include plays and sketches, music, tumbling and individual performances. All Troop members, (later including Cubs) had a chance to perform and were expected to sell tickets. Profits were used to benefit the Troop, especially when they were saving to improve their headquarters.

> 'I is …' began James, when his brother interrupted.
> 'That is wrong, you should say "I am".'
> 'All right', said James, 'I am the ninth letter of the alphabet.'
>
> *Traveller*: (Outside hotel) 'What's the matter, James, can't you get the engine to go?'
> *James*: 'It's that stupid ostler, sir, he's gone and given the petrol to the horse and put the oats in the motor.'

Jokes from the back page of Readiscout.

In 1937, the 1st Norwich gave a display of tumbling before a showing of the film of the Gang Show at the Carlton Picture Theatre.

Concerts, plays and entertainment continued to be popular activities for Scouts, especially at Christmas.

Community Service
Part of the ethos of Scouting is to help others. In the early days, Scouts were expected to look out for opportunities to help other people and to do at least one good turn every day. Continuing in this spirit, the Troop has always been willing to be of service to the community.

Fete at Colney Park
In 1921 Scouts helped at a fete at Colney Park held for the benefit of the Norfolk and Norwich Hospital. They patrolled the iron fencing near to the entrance to catch ticket

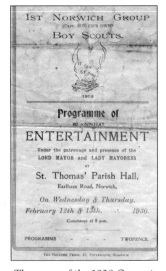
The cover of the 1930 Concert programme.

dodgers, looked after the parking enclosure for bicycles and cars, and sold programmes.

Parties for Widows and children

In the mid-1920s, the Troop undertook a Christmas good turn by providing dinner or gifts for twelve poor families.

Following this, they went on to organise larger Christmas parties for widows and children. One of these was held in Blackfriars Hall in 1930. It was run by the Scouts, under the control of the Children's Boarding Out Department, which was part of the Norwich Education Committee. The hall was given rent-free by permission of the Lord Mayor but the Scouts were responsible for out-of-pocket expenses such as heating and lighting.

Cub Christmas Show 1987. Leaders featured as characters from the popular T V programme Hi De Hi.

The Scouts did much of the work for the parties. Before the tables were laid they washed and dried the crockery, which came in straw-packed bales. They served at the tables, which were the full length of the hall, and afterwards, did the washing up and repacked the crockery. Rovers put on the entertainment including some lively slapstick comedy. Sandy Buttle says it was greeted with gales of laughter and some seventy years later, he can still feel the bruises he suffered during the performance.

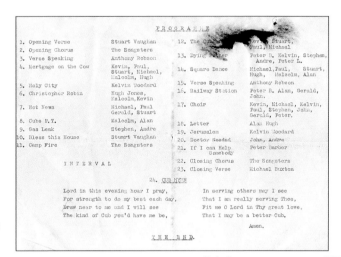

Cub Concert programme, 1958.

The Scouts were helped to arrange the parties by Miss Mary Grant, the Children Act Inspector for the Education Committee. She wrote to say how impressed she was by the work they did and when she died in 1969, she left the Troop a sum of money. This was used to purchase a glass-fibre boat, which they named the Lady Grant.

King George V Jubilee Beacon 1935

The Troop was made responsible for the King George V Jubilee Beacon on St James' Hill in 1935. An enormous bonfire, it was lit by the Lord Mayor, and reported to have been watched by over 10,000 people. Later, at the same site, Skipper Eric Greenfield was in charge of organising the Beacon to celebrate the Coronation of Queen Elizabeth II in 1953.

Bob-a-Job Week

This was an annual event held between 1914 and 1999. It started as Good Turn Week, became Bob-a Job Week in 1949 and was renamed Scout Job Week in 1970. During the week Scouts and Cubs would earn money for Group funds by

Good Turn dinner at Blackfriars Hall, 1925.

doing all sorts of jobs. In 1968 Scouts offered to sharpen old knives and scissors using an electric sharpener and in other years they set up a shoe-shine stall.

Building the Jubilee Beacon. St James' Hill, Norwich, 1935.

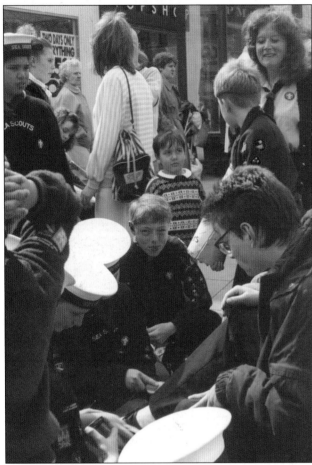

Scouts and Cubs shining shoes in the city centre. April 1992. Assistant Cub Leader, Jenny Smith back right.

Cub Leader, Charles Bartram, advertises the shoe shine on Hay Hill, Norwich, 1990.

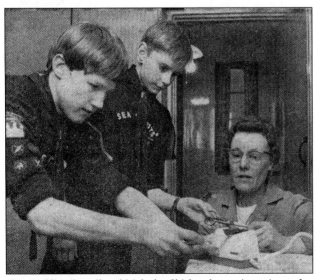

Scouts Clive Powell and Malcolm Shirley sharpening scissors for Mrs Kathleen Woodard during Bob-a-Job week, 1968.

Cubs in Action

Cub sport day, 1958.

Cubs perform the Nativity, Christmas 1959. Mary - Stephen Hunter, Joseph - Brian Riley, The Three Kings - Philip Green, Andrew Word, Stephen Moore, Arch Angel - Gerald Daniels, Small Angel - Peter Parnell.

Cub Sports Trophy winners, 1959.

Scouts: Kelvin Woodard and 'Ginger' Curtis canoeing with Cubs, c1959.

Scout Week, 1963.

Cubs with pumpkin lanterns at Halloween, 1977.

Cubs beside the wooden statue at Eaton Vale, 1988.

Cubs are shown the bees on their visit to 'Apple Bee' by bee keeper John Everett. 1984. Left to right: Mark Everett, Karl Diggens, Daniel Fitt, David Albury, Martin Faherty, Wayne Gardiner, Lee Harper, Andrew Watt, ?.

Left: Gold Six awarded at Hi De Hi Christmas concert, 1987. Cubs left to right: James Clements, Mark Fuller, Daniel Henry, Ian Slaughter, Christopher Smith.

Right: Whilst visiting the Norwich Castle dungeons, Cub Daniel Green gets the chance to try the 'ducking chair', 1993.

Left: The Cubs 'meet' Lord Baden-Powel at Madame Tussauds, March 1997.

Right: Cubs and Beavers come out of the players tunnel at Norwich City Football ground, c1997.

District Commissioner James Sinclair presents 1st Norwich Cubs with the 5-a-side winner's trophy, 1997.

On a trip to Legoland, c1999.

Pond dipping at Surlingham. Beaver Leader David Driver is helping at the event, c1999.

Visiting the Ted Ellis Trust at Surlingham, c1999. Kneeling left is Cub Leader Jane Stafford and extreme right is Alex Saunders, visiting from Belgium.

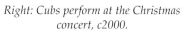

Left: Cub Will Walker gets to grips with the saw to obtain his Handymans Badge, c2000.

Right: Cubs perform at the Christmas concert, c2000.

125

Halloween time, 2001.

Pancake race, c2001.

Winners of the District Cooking Competition who went on to be one of two teams to represent the County of Norfolk in the Regional Final, 2006. Standing left to right: Daniel Gentle, Megan Rickards, Amelia Land, Ross Gilbert, Daniel Venn. Kneeling front: Katy Knights and Oliver Truswell.

The winners helped with refreshments at the 'Beacon of Promise' service, January, 2007.

Beavers on the Go

Fun at Family Camp, 1998.

Beavers at the Christmas Concert, c2000.

Visiting Banham Zoo, December 2001. Left to right: Alex Lloyd-Wickens, Jordon Newton, Callum Regan, Alex Holdsworth, Alex Shreeve, Charlie English, Lewis White and hiding at back, Connor Quarmby.

Visiting the Dinosaur Park, 2002.

Beavers with Asst. Cub Leader, Chris Regan at Banham Zoo. December 2001.

Group Fun Day, 2004.

Beaver sleep-over, 2004. Leaders: Joy Parfitt, kneeling left; Robert Hawes, centre back; Sara Cordy, right back.

Liam and Connor at the Fun Day, 2004.

Beaver pirates at sleep-over, 2004. Includes: Luke Annison, Oliver Truswell, Liam Healey, Ross Gilbert, Billy Farrow and Kyle Richardson.

Owen Cunningham and Daniel Robertson were winners of a county competition, and their prize was to join other winners for a day of football training at the Norwich City training ground, 2003.

Fund-raising

From the first days when Edward Coe and his friends pooled two thirds of their pocket money to buy equipment, fund-raising has always been on the agenda for the Group.

The necessity for good headquarters has often been the spur for fund-raising. Soon after the First World War the Troop was raising money to

The Group, January 1983.

enable them to extend their accommodation. A hut was purchased from an allotment holder for £12. A garden fete in 1918 and a social evening concert in 1920 helped to pay for the hut.

A garden fete at Earlham House in 1927 raised £50 to help with new headquarters.

In 1967 the present headquarters was financed by grants and loans. To repay the loan, weekly

SL Derek Page awaits customers on the 'Smash the Plate' stall, 1983.

bingo sessions (organised by Frank Folkard, Aleck Bartram and Arthur Rowe) became a popular source of income. In 1971 a wrestling match was arranged to help with repayment. Richard Goodrum recalls that Scouts towed a mirror dinghy on the back of a Bedford van

Scouts advertising the wrestling match, 1971.

through the streets of Norwich, ringing the Group's big brass ship's bell to advertise the event but records show that it didn't make a profit. Eric Greenfield reported a disappointing result financially ... *a good production with first class publicity and fine weather yet attendance was poor, resulting in a £10 loss.*

Favourite events for fund-raising have always been jumble sales, garden fetes, waste paper collections and dances. Recent years have seen a

Scout volunteers to be the 'wench' at the Drench the Wench stall, Summer fete, 1982.

A direct hit drenches the 'wench', 1982.

mixture of sponsored events such as cycle rides and abseiling. The writer (Jane) recalls being terrified of heights but agreed to abseil down the Scout Tower to kick-start the fund-raising for the Poland trip in 1994. It took her 30 minutes to pluck up courage to step off the ledge!

Sponsored cycle ride round the Lotus test track, May 1988.

'Quiz & Chips' nights and Fun Casino evenings have all proved to be good social events combined with raising funds.

The Group's most successful yearly fund-raising event, Jumbly, was launched in 1983 by Scout parent, Graham Pike. St Andrew's Hall was hired for the event and table space sub-let to other charities to cover the cost. The 1st Norwich were responsible for co-ordinating, advertising, entrance fee and refreshments. Cafe De Jumbly went on to become a huge success and made up a large part of the profit. The first year raised £435.25 for Group funds. Graham stepped down as organiser in 1993 and was given a Scouts Thanks Badge from the Group. Since Graham retired, the co-ordinator's position has been undertaken by Scout parents Pat Swinbourne, Angela Christopher, Sharon Smith and Annette Thomas. Over its now twenty-four year history, a conservative estimate would suggest this event has raised £20,000 for 1st Norwich Group funds with a further £100,000 having been raised by the various charities for their own causes.

Cub Scouts have played their part in fund-

raising. They undertook a sponsored silence to raise funds for Guide Dogs for the Blind, and in 1996 handed a cheque for £438 to the BBC's Children in Need appeal, having collected a mile of copper coins.

When the Group held its 90th Birthday re-union, Friends of the 1st Norwich was launched with the aim of raising £10,000 by the 100th Birthday in 2008. This target was reached in 2006, thanks to the generosity of past and present members.

Cub, Stewart Adcock displays the advertising poster for Jumbly, 1984.

When seven Scouts wanted to attend the 21st World Scout Jamboree in 2007, £7,000 had to be raised. They undertook a challenge to collect 100 kilos of copper money. They achieved this very quickly with the help of customers of Homebase, Hall Road, Norwich, raising £900. Bag packing at Sainsbury Superstore, Brazengate, proved a popular event with £535.00 raised. The target of £7,000 was achieved within nine months and all seven Scouts were able to attend the Jamboree.

The Fun in Fundraising will continue into the future, helping Scouts to achieve their aims and ambitions into the second century of the Group.

Sponsored abseil at HQ, September 1993. Left to right, standing: Keith and Jane Wincup, Elizabeth Culling, Pat Swinbourne, Jane Stafford. Kneeling: Miss Belton, Joy Parfitt.

Collecting 100 kilos of copper money at the Homebase store in Norwich, 2006. Left to right: Scouts Josee and Daniel, Asst. GSL Jane, Scouts Rachel, Lizzie and Mark, ASL Dean, Scout Alex.

ASL Tom Porteous starts the 'Duck race' a popular attraction at recent summer fetes. July 2006.

Summer Fete at Headquarters July 2006.

Lewis and Alex bag packing at Sainsburys, December 2006.

A Family Affair

It is not uncommon for families to have more than one member involved in the Scout Group. Some have had three or more often at the same time. Examples are:

Ted, Alfred and Carl Buttle (1928 to 1948).

Alan, Raymond, David and Brian Baxter (1940 to 1960s).

Brian, Malcolm, Trevor, Michael and Tony Buxton (1950s to 1960s).

James, Matthew and David Clements, along with their mum Glynnis, who was Beaver Scout Leader and dad Mick, who was a Parent Helper (1985 to the early 1990s).

Christopher, Hannah and Alex Smith and their mother Jenny who was an Assistant Cub Scout Leader(1985 to mid 1990s)

Douglas, Graham and Geraldine Hough (Mid 1990s)

Nathan, Jake, James and Connor Quarmby, and their dad, Sean, who was Beaver Scout Leader (1990s).

Oliver, Joseph and Amelia Rix (2008).

Elizabeth, Alex and Charlie Lloyd-Wickens (2008).

Ben, Megan and Zoe Rickards (2008).

Left: Four of the five Buxton brothers, who were in the Group at the same time. At the back, Brian. Middle row: left to right, Tony and Michael and at the front is Malcolm, c1960.

Below: Matthew, David and James Clements, 1988.

Assistant Cub Scout Leader sails in the Global Challenge 2004/05

The Cub Pack of 2004/2005 were able to follow, via the internet, the journey of one of their Cub Leaders, David Albury, when he swapped life in rural Norfolk for a 72ft ocean racing yacht, as he set off to sail around the globe in 'the world's toughest yacht race'. David was one of the 18 crew on the yacht BG Spirit in the Global Challenge 2004-05, racing 33,000 miles around the world against the prevailing winds and currents. David had been involved with the 1st Norwich Scout Group since he joined as a Cub in 1982, and for him, this journey was to fulfil a long held ambition.

The logs and courses were read and charted on a world map by the Cub Pack, for the 10 month duration of the race.

After leaving Portsmouth on the 3rd October in gale force winds, BG Spirit encountered the full spectrum of weather conditions from 60 knot winds with 50 foot waves to very light winds in the doldrums as they sailed south and across the Equator. After one particular storm, a damaged spinnaker sail took 160 man-hours to repair. Flying fish, a swarm of locusts and even showers of sand were encountered as the yacht sailed south. The Log reported 'huge rollers, waves breaking over the foredeck and smashing the crew trying to change sails, and lightning bolts lighting up the moonless night'. Later reports spoke of sailing in sunshine with temperatures of 40 degrees centigrade below decks.

The second leg of the race took the yachts around the infamous Cape Horn and into the Southern Ocean, which was everything David expected. The cold was intense and, with storms 'battering the yacht for days on end, life on board certainly became a challenge', yet they still managed to celebrate Christmas with re-hydrated roast chicken.

The third leg from Wellington to Sydney was a short sprint which saw BG Spirit leading the fleet into Sydney Harbour and crossing the finishing line opposite Sydney Opera House in first place.

After Sydney, it was back into the Southern Ocean again for leg four. During the race an email to supporters ashore spoke of helming the yacht in winds of over 45 knots, powering up and down waves that were 60 ft from crest to trough, with the southern lights playing in the skies above.

In leg five, the yachts returned to the Atlantic as they headed northwards again for Boston, USA. With a superb tactical move and their spinnaker sail flying most of the way, the crew returned to winning ways again, crossing the finish line in first place and one and a half

David Albury on the rigging 'rising to the challenge', 2005.

days and 243 nautical miles ahead of the next yacht. Crossing the Atlantic for a third time, the yachts turned towards home, heading first to La Rochelle in France for a quick stopover before the final sprint home.

With light winds forecast for the final leg back home to Portsmouth and a slim 5 point lead,

BG Spirit and crew tackle the rough seas, 2004.

it looked like being a cat and mouse chase up the English Channel with their two closest rivals, and a nail-biting time for the supporters back home. Instead, BG Spirit finished the race in style, winning the final leg as well as the overall race to receive the Princess Royal Trophy.

With champagne corks flying, the team were given a hero's welcome by the thousands of people, including family and friends, who had come down to Gunwharf Quays in Portsmouth to see their return. In turn, the 1st Norwich

Cubs were enthralled to hear David's account when he returned to Norwich.

David Albury gets to hold the winners' trophy, 2005.

Skipper Andy Forbes and crew are very pleased to receive the winners 'Princess Royal Trophy', from Sir Chay Blythe, 2005.

Scout Patrol Leaders 1908 - 2008

KANGAROO

1908-12	E H Coe *$#	1912-13	J Cordy	1913-14	W H Middleton *$#
1914-18	S C Spalding *$#	1918-19	G Priestly	1919	A Nutvhey
1919-21	N F Coe *$#	1921-24	D H Bullen	1924-25	J L Roberts *$
1925	J R Desborough	1926-28	J H Braybrooks *	1928-29	T W Killick *
1929	L J Palmer *	1929-32	S Dent	1932-34	K Abel
1934-35	H Todd	1935-36	A Buttle*	1936-37	J Gillingwater
1937-38	J Brown	1938-39	K Wilson	1939	M J Coe
1939-40	J Sadler	1940-42	C Pulford *	1942-43	P Wick
1943-44	C Buttle	1944-45	A Baxter	1945-46	G Hatch *
1946-48	S Pye	1948-50	D Baxter	1950-52	B Baxter
1952-53	A Betts	1953-55	M D Lemmon	1955-57	B E Hunn
1957	J King	1957-59	M Batson	1959-60	N Bobbit
1960-61	J Burrows	1961	M Buxton	1961-65	P Green
1965	P Jolly	1965-66	D Thurston	1967-68	J Roskell
1968-70	N Watson	1970	R Garrod	1970-71	A MacAllen
1971-72	C Garrod	1972-75	K Rowe	1975-77	M Thouless
1977-78	G Newson	1978-79	J Gascoyne	1979-80	C Moore
1980	C Newson	1980-81	A Keeley		

STAGS

1914-16	W H Middleton*#	1916-18	J L Osborne *	1918-19	C G Coleman
1919-24	A E Chance *$	1924-25	B G High *$	1925-26	S W Smith
1926-27	J Bobbit	1927-28	D W Brown	1928-29	G G Martin
1929-30	S C Braybrooks *	1930-31	E Huggins	1931	A M Abel
1931-32	B Reynolds	1932-33	R Herbert-Smith	1933-35	B Craske
1935-37	E Greenfield *#	1937	A Driver	1937-38	A Brown
1938-40	R Harcourt	1940-41	P Beamis	1941-42	P Martin *
1942-43	P Howell	1943-44	D Smith	1944-45	W Bloomfield
1945-48	A Cooper	1948-50	B Moore	1950-52	J Webster
1952-53	P Gibbs	1953-55	M Lyon	1955-56	J Palmer
1956-57	M Palmer	1957-59	T Buxton	1959-60	J Curtis
1960-61	A Adcock *$	1961-63	P Easy	1963-64	M Beart
1964-65	D Pointer	1965-67	K Rowe* $	1967-68	C Bartram *$
1968-69	M Shirley	1969-70	W Fischer	1971-72	P Brighton
1972-73	K High	1973-75	S Green	1975-76	J Poynter
1976-78	C Lindsey	1978-79	M Ray	1980-81	M Weinle
1981-82	N Nixon	1982	S Carver	1982	M Victor
1982	P Rychmovsky	1983	K Robertson	1983-84	P Rychnovsky
1984-85	A Pike	1985-87	J Pike	1987-89	D Albury
1989-91	S Adcock	1991	P Cutting	1996	L. Allen
1996-98	W Perry	1999	J Cannors	2002	P Robertson
2003-04	J Palmer	2004-05	S Penny	2005-06	A Mitchell
2006	J Perkins	2006-08	M Palmer	2008	J Reeve

BEAVERS (Patrol name change from Stags, reverted back in 1996)

1993 -	C Boden	1994-95	S Ainsworth	1995-96	J Green

SEAGULL

1926-27	J Watling	1927-29	J H Braybrooks *	1929-30	T W Killock
1930-31	G G Martin	1931-32	S C Braybrooks	1932-33	A Abel
1933-34	H Hansen	1934-35	C J Martins	1935	M Palmer
1935	J H Howard	1935-37	H Todd	1937-38	B Craske
1938-39	J Gillingwater	1939-42	F Folkard	1942-43	C Pulford
1943-45	J Tuttle				

DRAKE

1949-50	B Mason	1950-52	D Baxter	1952-56	J Webster
1956-57	P Gibbs				

RALEIGH

1950	S Moore

HAWK

1923-24	F F Smith	1924-26	J Watling *	1926-27	D Young
1927-28	N Porter	1928-29	G Want	1929-30	H Clarke
1930-31	H Hanson	1931-32	A Batch	1932-33	M Palmer
1933-34	J H Howard	1934	J West	1934-35	A Buttle
1935-37	F Batch	1937	W Mildrd	1937-38	L Aldridge
1938-39	G Flint	1939-41	H Peek	1941-42	K Mallett
1942-43	C Carter	1943-44	B Brown	1944-45	P Bowen
1945-48	N Gilman	1948-50	B Mason	1950-52	J Aldridge
1952-55	L Aldridge	1955-57	J O'Dell	1957-58	B Buxton
1958-60	J Grimmer	1960-61	D Ovens	1961-62	M Braithwaite
1963-64	S Vaughen	1964-67	C Powell	1967-68	R Revell
1968-70	R Claxton	1970-71	C Green	1971-72	D Fischer
1972-73	G Sherwood	1973-74	R Robinson	1974-76	S Saul
1975-76	R Goodrum	1976-77	L Hill	1977-79	D Rose
1979-80	N Nixon	1980-82	D Stapleton	1982-83	M Barley
1983-84	A Pike	1988-89	P Woods	1989-90	D Kleiweg
1990-93	J Clements	1993-94	J Ambrozevich	1995-96	L Bargewell
1996-97	D Tink	1997	A Godfrey	1999	T Smith
2002	R. Wincup	2003	C Palmer	2004-06	E Lloyd-Wickens
2006-07	G Beaumont	2007-08	O Rix	2008	A Elliott

OWL

1922-23	C Gossling	1923-24	W T Barber *$	1924-25	E W Martin
1925-27	J Watling *	1927-28	C Driver	1931-32	C Hunt

LION

1908-10	L Glover	1919-20	R Coltman	1920-22	S Cracknell
1959-69	R Pennington	1960-61	P White *	1961-62	M Gilmore
1962-63	K Goldsmith	1963-64	K Woodard *	1964-65	C Moore
1965-66	M Gardener	1967-68	J Sayer	1968-70	K Fisher
1970-71	R Crane	1971-72	C Bartram *	1972-73	D Gibbon
1973-74	G Sherwood	1974-76	S Dunbar	1976-77	I Mountain
1977-79	J Packer	1979-80	S Hobbs	1980-81	C Solt
1981-83	N Grogutt *	1985-86	S Crew	1986-87	M Spencer
1989-90	R Smith	1990-91	C Smith	1992-94	K Adcock*$
1994-95	A Bargewell	1996-97	T Christopher	1997-	L Carter
1999	S Culling*	2002	L Cubbage	2003-05	W Saunders
2005-06	M Robertson*	2006-	C Lodge	2007-	G Beaumont

BADGER

1914-15	J Higgs	1915-17	N Cooper	1917-18	R S Dye
1978-79	A Cullington	1979-80	A Waite	1980	V Roper
1980-81	S Mace	1984-85	J Pitcher	1985	P Davies
1986	S Crew	1987	D Turnham	1987-89	D Wilcox *
1989-90	I Blackburn	1990-91	M Balls	1991-92	C Newitt
1993-94	D Hough	1994-95	T Porteous*	1996-97	D Perry
1997-98	L Godfrey	1999	R Lodge	2002	G Culling
2003-05	A Robinson	2005	D Anderton	2005-06	F Shephard
2006-07	A Saunders	2007	R Mills	2007	L White

CURLEW

1918-19	A Palmer	1919-20	C A Andrews	1917-18	E Burroughes

FAWN

1922-24	B G High

WALLABY

1923-24	J L Roberts

WOLF

1915-16	H Roberts	1916-17	G Potter

OTTER

1912-13	W Bishop	1913-14	W Cox *	1914-17	N S Dye
1917-18	P Palmer	1918-19	W Pearce	1919	S Cracknell
1919-20	L Lodge	1920-22	R Boatwright		

Subsequent Warrant Holder $ Subsequent Wood Badge Holder   # Subsequent Commissioner.

Past and Present Leaders of the 1st Norwich Sea Scout Group

GROUP SCOUT LEADERS

1928-47	Edward Coe	1947-50	John Seymour
1950-73	Eric Greenfield	1973 to date	Alan Adcock

ASSISTANT GROUP SCOUT LEADER

2002 to date   Jane Stafford

SCOUT LEADERS

	Scout Masters/Leaders		Assistant Scout Masters/Leaders
1909	Claude Stratford	1913	Mr Loades & Mr Bennett
1912-17	Charles F. Bower	1914	Edward Coe, John Mosby & W. Cox
1915	Arthur T Nicholls (Honorary SM during WWI)	1916	William Middleton (acting ASM)
1917-28	Edward Coe (Appointed SM on the death of Charles Bower)	1917	John Mosby, DSO, W Cox, William Midleton, S Spalding
1921	John Mosby DSO (Acting SM while Edward Coe was studying in London)		
		1927	Mr Roberts and W T Barber
		1928	A E Chance (also acting Rover Leader) W T Barber, Philip Thoulass & J Watling
1932	Dr John Mosby		
1930s	A E Batch		
1937-39	John Bracey		
1939-60s	J Tuttle		
1945-46	Mr Seymour (Acting SM)		
1948-59	Mr Pulford		
c1950	Frank Folkard		
1947	Eric Greenfield		
1950s	Basil Craske		
1950s	James White (Pilot)		
1965-69	Dalmaine Dewgarde	1965-69	Brian Buxton & Eddie Goldsmith
1966-68	Peter White		
1965-67	Kelvin Woodard		
1971	Alan Adcock	1971	Mike Clarke
1973	Keith Rowe	1973	Dave Reyner
		c1975	David Beckett
		1977	Julian Greenfield
1980	Derek Page		
1980-83	Martin LeGrice	1980-83	Dave Walford
1990-91	Richard Cosburn		
1991-95	Julien Pike		
1995 to date	Julian Greenfield		
		1997-2002	Danny Willcox
		1988 to date	Neil Grogutt
		1999 to date	Tom Porteous
		2002	Liz Ainsworth & Helen Grogutt
		2001 to date	Katie Adcock
		2003 to date	Dean Ward
		2006 to date	Mark Elvin
		2004-08	Becky Adcock

TROOP LEADERS

1919-20	S R Clarke	1920-21	J D Hick
1921-24	N F Coe	1924-27	W T Barber
1927-31	D V Young	1931-33	A M Abel
1933-34	R Herbert-Smith	1934-35	K Abel
1935-37	H Todd	1937	E Greenfield
1937-39	J Gillingwater	1939-41	L Batson
1941-43	C Pulford	1943-44	P Martin
1944-45	B Browne	1945	W Bloomfield
1952-53	A Betts	1953-54	R Wright
1957	J O'Dell		

VENTURE & EXPLORER SCOUT LEADERS

Venture Scout Leaders

c1965-77	Dave Reyner
c1966-77	Eddy Goldsmith
c1975	Ray Crisp
c1980-95	Derek Page
c1996	Mark Green
c1997	Jill Austin

Explorer Scout Leaders		**Assistant Explorer Scout Leaders**	
2002-06	Danny Wilcox	2002-06	Helen Grogutt
2006 to date	Shaun Culling	2007-08	Nicky Bensted-Smith

CUB SCOUT LEADERS

Cub Scout Masters/Leaders		**Assistant Cub Scout Masters/Leaders**	
1920	Miss Mary Easton (Cub Mistress)	1921	Alfred E Palmer
1923	William Middleton	1927	B G High
1928	Neville Coe	1932	Philip Thouless
c1948-52	Alan Baxter		
1952-58	Fred Jones (Bos'un)	1952-58	Miss Ann Grix
1958-63	Miss Dinah Higham	1958-63	Mary Palmer
		1961	Gillian Williams
1964-67	Mrs Ratcliff	1964-67	Lynette Greenfield
1968-78	Mrs Fischer	1964-78	Charles Bartram
1978 to date	Charles Bartram	1978-79	Mrs Maureen Staff
		1979	Martin Thouless
		1982	Sheila Holmes
		1986-99	Jane Stafford (nee Blyth)
		1988	Jenny Smith
		1995-04	David Albury
		2000-04	Mary Anderton
		2002-05	Francis Taylor (Young Leader)
		2004 to date	Alison Buck
		2005 to date	Christopher Regan
		2007 to date	Tom Egleton (Helper)
		2007 to date	Andy Daly (Helper)
		2008 to date	Mark Robertson (Young Leader)

BEAVER SCOUT LEADERS

	Beaver Scout Leaders		Assistant Beaver Scout Leaders
1988-93	Glynnis Clements (started the Beaver Colony at first with guidance from Jane Stafford)	1989-93	Ruth Boden
1993-95	Ruth Boden	1993	Rosie Evans
1995-96	Elizabeth Culling	1995-96	Debbie Wilson
1996	Debbie Wilson		
1996-99	Sean Quarmby	1996-99	David Driver
1998-99	Mary Anderton		
1999-2000	David Driver	2000 to date	Robert Hawes
2001	Robert Hawes (With help from Jane Stafford ADC)		
2001 to date	Joy Parfitt		
		2004 to date	Sara Cordy
		2007 to date	Alison MacNab
		2008 to date	Kalani Rhodes
		2008 to date	Samatha Rose

The dates above indicate, as far as is known, the year a Leader took on the role under which his/her name is listed and for how long they remained in that role. Information has been based on the somewhat scant and piecemeal records available in the archive and recollections of past and present Group members. For these reasons, there are bound to be inaccuracies in the names, dates and titles given. Apologies are extended to all those who may be wrongly represented or even missed altogether.

List of Contributors

Stewart Adcock
David Albury
Lenny Aldridge
Brian Baxter
David Baxter
John Bracey
Malcolm Braithwaite
John Burroughs
Alfred Buttle, (Sandy)
Carl Buttle
Brian Buxton
Glynnis Clements
Andrew Coe
Maurice Cornelius
Kate Dulieu
Derek Evans
Peter Gibb
Richard Goodrum
Lynette Greenfield
John Grimmer

Helen Grogutt
Rosslyn Hall
Hayden Hardy
Gordon Hatch
Gillian Jeckells
Mary LeWinton, (nee Palmer)
Mike Lyon
Ian Mountain
Janet Mountain
John Nelson
Derek Page
Keith Rowe
Joyce Sillett
Jenny Smith
Hanna Smith
Chris Smith
Georgina Thomas
Peter White
Kelvin Woodard
David Woods

Tribute is paid to Bert Batch, Alan Baxter, Peter Dearn, Frank Folkard, Dick Harcourt and Albert Pye who also contributed to the book but sadly have not lived to see its publication.

Other Sources

1st Norwich Sea Scout Group Archive, Norfolk Record Office
Edward Coe, Memoirs
Lord Baden Powell, Scouting for Boys, Thirty-Second Edition, 1960. C Arthur Pearson Ltd.

Internet Sources

'Johnny' Walker's Scouting Milestones, www.scouting.milestones.btinternet.co.uk, accessed January 2008.
The Scout Association Website, www.scoutbase.org.uk, accessed October 2007.
James Arthur Rose, BBC WW2 Peoples War, www.bbc.co.uk/ww2peopleswar/stories, accessed July 2007.

Abbreviations

ABSL, Assistant Beaver Scout Leader

ACSL, Assistant Cub Scout Leader

ADC, Assistant District Commissioner

AESL, Assistant Explorer Scout Leader

AGSL, Assistant Group Scout Leader

ASL, Assistant Scout Leader

AVSL, Assistant Venture Scout Leader

BSL, Beaver Scout Leader

CEYMS, Church of England Young Men's Society

CSL, Cub Scout Leader

Capt., Captain

DC, District Commissioner

DSO, Distinguished Service Order

ES, Explorer Scout

ESL, Explorer Scout Leader

GSL, Group Scout Leader

GSM, Group Scout Master

HQ, Headquarters

MC, Military Cross

PL, Patrol Leader

RS, Rover Scout

RSS, Rover Sea Scout

RSSM, Rover Sea Scout Mate

RSSSec., Rover Sea Scout Second

S, Scout

SL, Scout Leader

SM, Scout Master

SS, Senior Scout

SSPL, Senior Scout Patrol Leader

TL, Troop Leader

VS, Venture Scout

VSL, Venture Scout Leader